SONG OF THE SECOND FIDDLE

SONG *of the* SECOND FIDDLE

Todd Hahn

HORIZON BOOKS

CAMP HILL, PENNSYLVANIA

HORIZON BOOKS
3825 Hartzdale Drive, Camp Hill, PA 17011
www.cpi-horizon.com
www.christianpublications.com

Song of the Second Fiddle
ISBN: 0-88965-179-5

LOC Control Number: 00-131985

Printed in the United States of America

00 01 02 03 04 5 4 3 2 1

Contents

Preface

This book is for those who are called by God to be followers and want to do it the best they can. It is for those who are followers and are tired of following. It is for those who aren't sure if they are a follower or a leader. It is for those who question if there is any value to being a follower. And it is for leaders who want to learn how to relate to their followers in richer ways.

I hope it is not too grandiose to say that this book is for all of us, because all of us follow in some area of our lives. This book is written by a Christ-follower for Christ-followers, but if you are not a follower of Christ, I hope the book will give you a taste of what it might mean to follow a Leader who loves you with His whole heart. Maybe you will be tempted to want to become a follower of Christ. I hope so.

I am grateful to my team of co-followers on the Warehouse 242 staff—Marc Dickmann, Jennifer Hibbert, Jenny Lewis and Stacy Pickerell. They make it easy and fun to be a leader. Stacy even let me write most of the book at her house while she was working; fortunately, she works long hours! Over the last five years, I have watched Stacy exemplify effective followership on the highest level. I also am grateful for her intuition that life is no more or no less than a high-stakes chess game.

I am also grateful to the stellar leadership team of Warehouse, who model much of what I write about in this book and who graciously insist that I take time to write and speak.

Jane, Justin and Jonathan have responded with love and support to my leadership and are the most important followers in my life.

Most of all, I am grateful to Jesus, who allows me to follow Him. Thank You, Lord, for serving me and allowing me the stunning, breathtaking and wholly undeserved privilege of following You. Help me to follow You with all of my heart, soul, mind and strength.

Part One

The Challenge of Following

Chapter

1

The Myth of Leadership

Bill put his arm around Steve and squeezed, leaned close to Steve's ear and whispered, "Do you have any idea how lucky you are to get to work for Pastor Tom? To have a mentor like him at this point in your career, a man who is so gifted and godly? Plenty of young pastors would kill for the opportunity you have!" As he always did, Steve agreed with the elder's expression of faith in Tom.

"You're right, Bill," he replied. "It really is a privilege to be Tom's associate pastor, and I'm grateful to God for the opportunity."

Bill smiled and loosened his grip on Steve's shoulder. "Keep remembering that, Steve, and make sure that you help Pastor Tom to carry his load. A lot of us depend on him and love him. Some of us owe our lives to his ministry. We're counting on you to take care of him and to support him so that he can be and do all that God has called him to. Keep up the good work!"

When Bill had left Steve's office, the young pastor exhaled a long breath, rubbed his eyes, kicked his feet up on his desk and drummed his fingers on the back of his neck. Just a bit impatiently.

I know he's right—they're all right, Steve thought. *Tom is a great guy, tremendously gifted and called by God. He's a great leader and preacher, and he inspires confidence in lots of people. It really is an incredible opportunity to direct Christian education and student ministries for his church. And I know that one of the reasons I'm at this church is to support him and encourage him.*

But it's hard to always be seen as the young, supportive, number-two guy in the shadows. Just once, I'd like somebody to affirm my gifts, to tell me that I'm important in my own right, to tell me that I matter and that I'm more than just a supportive backdrop for Tom's ministry.

Steve spun around in his chair, faced his office window and shook his head to clear his thoughts. *But the fact is, that's not going to happen. I'm just not as important as he is and I've got to face that. I'll have to find affirmation where I can, from myself and from the Lord, and just soldier on. Maybe if I serve Tom well, I will get my own chance to lead someday. That may take forever, but I guess that's what endurance is all about. That's the best I can hope for now.*

The Myth Takes Shape

Steve is well-meaning, sincere, committed to his leader and full of integrity. He is also setting himself up for disillusionment, heartbreak and a far less effective ministry than he might have. Steve has bought into the myth of leadership.

The myth of leadership is this: *Leaders are more important than followers, and every other spiritual role or activity is inferior to leadership.* Implicit in the myth is the belief that followers are, at best, tools in the hands of a gifted leader and, at worst, potential obstacles to the realization of a leader's plans and goals. The myth of leadership creates a two-tiered world. On the narrow top ledge are the very few gifted and called leaders. The rest of us occupy a vast plain somewhere below—nameless, faceless, insignificant followers.

> The myth of leadership is this: *Leaders are more important than followers.*

Those who study and think about leadership often trace our understanding of leadership through different eras. In the "Great Man Era" of leadership theory, for example, we believed that leaders were born rather than made and that their inherent leadership ability came to the surface when faced with a great crisis. Later, our thinking about leadership broadened and extended into the "Trait Era," when we tried to identify the inherent and developed qualities and characteristics of leaders. Later eras of leadership theory have noted the parts that behavior, external circumstances and changing social climates play in leadership.

All of these discussions of leadership have one thing in common: *They focus almost exclusively on the leader and ignore those whom the leader is supposed to be leading.* We think, write and argue much about leadership. Followership is more often than not lost in the shuffle.

Our culture, especially our Christian culture, tends to glorify the leader and the leader's activities. We admire those who are able to assess a situation accurately and can focus people and resources to move an organization forward. We praise those who have that elusive thing called vision and are able to rally others to see the same things they do. We try to emulate those who have built strong, growing, resourceful companies, organizations, ministries and churches. We respect those who can command, especially those who cause us to want to follow them.

But we don't pay so much attention or respect to those who follow well, to those who serve leaders by helping the leaders' visions and goals become reality. Leadership is cherished, sought after and honored. Followership is assumed, avoided at times and usually taken for granted.

"In our culture," says writer Ira Chaleff, "being a follower connotes weakness, passivity, or mindlessness."[1]

Joseph Rost goes into more detail, arguing that, historically, followers have been understood to be those who were part of the sweaty masses and therefore separated from the elites, were not able to act intelligently without the guidance and control of others, were willing to let others take control of their lives and were unproductive unless directed by others.[2]

Maybe You, but Not Me!

Another aspect of the myth of leadership is the assumption that leaders are not followers. Often, we assume that the roles are exclusive of one another and even unrelated. Many strong leaders do not think of themselves as followers. If they have worked and sacrificed to attain their position of leadership, many leaders feel as if followership is little more than a necessary part of their past. Now they are free to move on to the important business of being a leader.

A moment's reflection, though, shows that virtually every leader is also a follower. Even leaders in the most influential positions report to someone. A president or chief executive reports to his board of directors. A powerful senior pastor reports to a board of elders or deacons or to denominational officials. Even leaders who are not under the oversight of a board (an unenviable position, in fact) are accountable to government laws and standards. The most powerful leader can be stopped by a rookie highway patrolman!

It is a myth that leaders are above the mundane discipline of followership. Everyone follows someone, sometime.

Following the Leader

As is so often the case, the Bible turns cultural assumptions upside down. Our culture emphasizes leadership and its attendant perks, prestige and power. The Bible emphasizes followership and its attendant sacrifices, obscurity and servanthood. While the Bible does speak often and insistently about leadership, it speaks much more about the quiet demands of being a follower.

It is a myth that leaders are above the mundane discipline of followership. Everyone follows someone, sometime.

The Old Testament's emphasis on following is nearly impersonal; like an undercurrent, the people of God are instructed to follow His commands, decrees and laws (Leviticus 18:4, 20:8; Deuteronomy 30:8; 1 Kings 6:12). To follow is simply to obey from the heart. Great blessing is promised to those who follow the word of the Lord (Deuteronomy 4:1, 11:22-24) and serious curses for those who refuse to follow God or who follow other gods (Deuteronomy 6:14-15, Jeremiah 7:6, 9). The psalmists, in particular, beg God to give them a heart to follow after His word (Psalm 119:33, 63, 106, 166).

Followership in the New Testament, however, becomes strikingly and immediately personal. Jesus' first recorded public words are an invitation to follow Him. "Follow me," he says to Peter and Andrew, "and I will make you fishers of men." Their response is immediate: "At once they left their nets and followed him" (Matthew 4:19-20). The first chapters of Matthew, which record the beginning of Jesus' public ministry, are peppered with similar calls to follow Jesus. Nowhere in these passages does Jesus call people to believe anything or to accept anything. His appeal is simple, urgent and direct: Stop whatever it is that you are doing and follow Me without reservation.

Matthew, Mark and Luke deepen the call to follow by recording these words of Jesus: "Anyone who does not carry his cross and follow me cannot be my disciple" (Luke 14:27). To follow in the New Testament means to follow a *person*; it is a serious business that may well cost the followers their lives.

There is a consistency between the Old and New Testament appeals to follow. In the Old Testament, the emphasis is on following the word of God—His commands, laws and decrees. The New Testament emphasizes following the Word of God—the Person of Jesus, who Himself is the Author and Creator and summation of all of God's words.

To be a Christian is to be a *Christ-follower*—a term I will use throughout this book. To be a Christian is, before anything else, to be a follower, regardless of the leadership positions and responsibilities one may hold.

The myth of leadership suggests that leadership is of paramount importance and that leaders are to be honored more than followers. The Bible, by contrast, says that a life that brings joy to God is the life of a follower. All of us are followers before we are anything else. The myth begins to unravel.

Living without the Myth

Losing cherished assumptions is both difficult and exhilarating. It is hard to let go of something we have long believed because life seems a bit less certain and predictable, our place in the order of things a little less clear-cut. But it is also exciting to clear the ground because we gain a new understanding of who we are and we are given new opportunities for growth.

For those of us who are leaders, the death of the leadership myth may be hard to swallow at first. We have become accustomed to our position, and it is not easy to learn another role, especially one we thought we had outgrown. But to become a follower as well as a leader can be a freeing thing as well, liberating us from the belief that we have to know, do and manage all things on our own.

If we are followers, the death of the leadership myth may be difficult to accept because it can be a safe place to be sheltered underneath the wings of a leader whom we trust. To stretch beyond that may seem to be asking too much. On the other hand, the death of the myth means that we can understand ourselves and the role of follower to which God has called us in a new, more focused light. Perhaps there is value in being a follower after all.

Followers and leaders are both important actors in a drama; both influence the other and both are indispensable.

When a myth dies, truth has to replace it. I am advocating that the truth of the dynamic challenge of followership replace the myth of leadership. This truth is dynamic because it is active and interactive. Followers and leaders are both important actors in a drama; both influence the other and both are indispensable. Followers and leaders need each other. Together, they make a whole.

In human terms, however, leaders may need followers more than followers need leaders. "Leaders only really accomplish something by permission of the followers," says the wise business executive and writer Max DePree.[3] The great majority of us are called to follow others. Only to the extent that we follow well—with passion, integrity and excellence—will the visions of our leaders, the best of them given by God, be realized.

"Leadership and followership," writes Ira Chaleff, "are two parts of one dynamic relationship."[4] What unites and brings the two together is a broader commitment to a common purpose that gives meaning, dignity and connection to the relationship. The leader-follower relationship is not about the leader; a follower does not exist simply to serve the leader. The balance of this book will argue that there is great value in followership for its own sake, because followership captures the core of Christian character, serves God's purposes in an organization and models the countercultural values of God's kingdom. If we are Christ-followers, we will want to know what it means to be a follower and how we can follow better.

What Followership Is Not

It is often easier to understand what something is by seeing clearly what it is not. *Followership is not subservience.* Subservience is an ugly word that means to be less than a servant. A subservient relationship is one in which the weaker party blindly accepts the dictates of the stronger without thinking, challenging or employing creativity. In a subservient relationship, the stronger party fails to honor the dignity and worth of the weaker. The weaker one is simply a dispensable tool to accomplish the purposes of the strong one.

Jesus rejects any such relationship of subservience. He especially warns leaders against enforcing subservience on followers. When His disciples began to argue about which one of them was the greatest, Jesus slammed them: "The kings of the Gentiles lord it over them; and those who exercise authority over them call themselves Benefactors. But you are not to be like that. Instead, the greatest among you should be like the youngest, and the one who rules like the one who serves" (Luke 22:24-26). In biblical relationships, the roles of leader and follower are often interchangeable. It is never acceptable for one person to be a tool of another. Any follower in such an abusive relationship which continues over time should leave the relationship as soon as possible.

Followership is not subservience, but it is very much servanthood. Servanthood in followership is so critical that we will devote a whole chapter to it. For now, it is enough to say that the role of the servant is considered by Jesus to be the highest calling of all. Followers are very much to be servants of their leaders. Servants, not slaves.

Followership is not passivity. A follower that never challenges, questions or prods does a disservice to the leader. The myth of leadership suggests that leaders know best in every instance. In fact, followers, by virtue of their nearness to the details of the organization, may well know more than does the leader about a given issue. Followers serve the leader and the mission of the organization when they insist that the leader hear and respond to their concerns.

Jody is a young manufacturer's rep for a cosmetics company. One of the company's largest clients, a chain of department stores, has always been very demanding, especially in terms of cost and delivery schedule. Lately, however, the client has been more insistent than usual that Jody give them special discounts and rapid delivery of product.

Jody shared these developments with her boss, who cut her story off and said curtly: "These guys have been customers for years and know that we give them the best deal they can get. They like to rattle our cages a little. Just ignore them, keep to our usual pricing structure and delivery schedule and ride it out."

But Jody felt intuitively that there was something amiss with the client relationship. She argued that she should sit down with the client, just to insure that the relationship was on solid footing and that there weren't any factors Jody's company didn't know about. But Jody's boss didn't agree. "You don't have time to hold their hands," he said. "Go out and get new business and let those guys bark at the moon. They'll come around." So Jody did nothing.

This morning, Jody met with the client at his request. To her shock, he informed her that he was giving his business to a leading competitor of Jody's company. "They are offering us a substantial discount under your prices," the client said. "Plus, they just seem to care more."

Jody carried out the dictates of her boss, mostly without question. She did what he wanted, but her passivity resulted in the loss of one of her company's biggest clients, the source of her largest commission check.

Effective followers realize that the relationship between follower and leader is a dynamic one. The leader possesses ultimate authority, to be sure, but the follower also bears responsibility to make sure that the leader has all of the information and perspective he or she needs to make right decisions.

Far from being passive, good followers ask questions. Some questions followers should ask themselves about their leaders include:

- Can I trust this person to have not only the organization's best interests at heart, but mine as well?
- Will this person maintain a standard worthy of following?
- Can I expect this person to always be honest with me?

Some helpful, appropriate questions followers should ask of their leaders include:

- How do you maintain a life consistent with the values and vision of the organization?
- If I have a problem with the ethics or morality of a course of action, are you open to discussing it?
- How does the mission of our organization fit in with the purposes of God?
- Is God being honored by what we are doing?
- Do our activities represent good stewardship of the resources which God has given us?

- Do I have the freedom to pursue God's call on my life under your leadership?

Insecure leaders are threatened by questions such as these. This danger is especially real in Christian ministries or churches where it is assumed that the leader exclusively hears from God. An insecure leader is apt to suggest that any questioning of the leader is equivalent to questioning God.

An insecure leader is apt to suggest that any questioning of the leader is equivalent to questioning God.

But secure leaders thrive on such questions and are quick to provide answers. The very best leaders, in fact, create a mission-focused, personally supportive climate that all but eliminates the need for such questions.

Good followers are not passive, but they are supportive. They know the vision and values of the organization and the leader before they join the team, and are faithful to live up to those values and to support the leader in his or her task. Followers can create security in the heart of the leader by showing that they are fully invested in the organization, committed to honesty and integrity, sharp enough to challenge the process and responsive to the leader's initiative. Ultimately, a follower will leave an organization rather than undermine a godly leader with whom the follower happens to disagree.

Such trust takes time to build, but the trust-building process creates a climate where the leader can hear and respond to the concerns and opinions of the follower. Effective followers are supportive without being passive.

Finally, *followership is not a waiting game.* Many followers, such as Steve in the story which opened this chapter, are enduring followership because they are holding out for a position of leadership and influence down the line.

There is a fine line here. Every good leader has first been prepared by being a good follower. Followership can and often does pave the way for leadership. And it is wise for a follower who senses a call to future leadership to take advantage of his or her time as a follower to prepare and ask hard questions about leadership. A full chapter of this book is devoted to this issue.

But future leaders must always fight against the attitude that followership is time spent toiling in the "minor leagues" which one has to endure for a time before moving up to the "majors" of leadership. This belief undermines the dignity and importance of being a follower and evidences a lack of contentment in the heart of the follower.

Following "until something better comes along" also distracts the follower from the hard work of supporting and encouraging the leader. To follow well—to do anything well—requires commitment and dedication in the moment, a relentless determination to seize every opportunity afforded by the here and now. An effective follower gives everything for the cause, the leader and the organization, holding nothing in reserve. This kind of dedication is not possible when a follower is just marking time until the real game—leadership—begins.

The Challenge Begins

So followership is not subservience, passivity or a waiting game. Followership is part of a dynamic relationship and has great value in itself. What does it mean for us to be followers in the details of our lives? How can we follow more effectively? Just what does an effective follower do? What do we do when leadership goes bad? How can we take advantage of the opportunities and avoid the pitfalls of followership? The balance of this book examines these questions. We begin first by looking at those followers who have preceded us and have modeled meeting the challenge of followership.

Endnotes

1. Ira Chaleff, "Effective Followership." *Executive Excellence,* April, 1996, p.16.
2. Joseph Rost, *Leadership for the Twenty-First Century* (Westport, CT: Greenwood, 1991), p. 107.
3. Max DePree, *Leadership Jazz* (New York: Dell, 1992), p. 201.
4. Chaleff, p. 16.

Chapter

2

The Dilemma of Ambition

"All the potential in the world"—that was the phrase that described Ross. He had always had a sense of destiny. As long as he could remember, he just knew somehow that God had made him to accomplish great things, to lead large groups of people, to leave a movement in his wake.

Ross was unusually gifted and had a magnetic personality, and so others assumed as well that he would become something special. As he moved through college, several years of experience in the marketplace and then into professional ministry, he was viewed at every place as someone to keep an eye on, someone who would probably go on to significant influence.

Over time, Ross' journals and prayers became preoccupied with finding his place of destiny. His heart, the best he could tell, was for God and what God was doing in the world, but Ross found it hard to separate God's work from his own life.

The leader of the mission agency for which Ross worked was a kind, gentle, unassuming man. Not very gifted or eloquent, nor a particularly penetrating thinker, Bill had followers because of his humility and track record of hearing and responding to God in a way that paid off for the organization. While Ross respected Bill, over time he began to chafe under what he considered his boss' "directionless and uninspired" leadership. In Ross' mind, the new realities of ministry in a postmodern culture required, over the long haul, a different set of skills than God had given Bill. A set of skills, thought Ross, with a valiant effort to maintain humility, that he himself had.

As Ross was praying and journaling one morning, the true orientation of his heart became clear in a way it never had before. He wanted to be the leader of the mission; he believed that he could do a better job than Bill, now and for the future. He loved the organization and its vision, and he really wanted to see its success. What he realized now was how much he saw its success tied in with his own life.

Ross exhaled slowly and leaned back in his recliner. "This is a big moment for me," he realized. "I know what I think and what I want. What I have to decide now is what to do with it."

Many followers have to grapple at some point with the reality of personal ambition. We desire promotion, recognition, expanded influence and greater responsibility. Often, if we're honest, we desire leadership over our leaders because we think we could do a better job than they are doing.

When the struggle with ambition comes—and it most likely will—we will face the same moment of decision as Ross did. We have to decide what to do with our ambitious desires, how to act or not act in response to them. Our decision reveals quite a bit about our heart.

> Ambition can be good or destructive; it all depends on what direction it pulls us—toward God's purposes or our own.

One way to respond is to let ambition have its way. This is certainly acceptable in our culture. Even with a commitment to maintain high ethical standards and play within the rules, there are a number of things we can do to insure that we are well-positioned within our organization, that we are known by the decision-makers and that our work stands out from that of our colleagues. We can expend a lot of time and energy playing games like these and, whether we like it or not, we have to admit that they often work.

On the other hand, we can try to exorcize the first fleeting thoughts of ambition, assuming that any ambition is not from God and reflects a selfish heart. We can go out of our way to fade into the background, avoid promotion and recognition, and do everything we can not to stand out from our peers.

Neither response to the reality of ambition is biblical or healthy. Ambition can be good or destructive; it all depends on how we respond to it and what direction it pulls us—toward God's purposes or our own.

When Ambition Goes Bad

We'll talk about the upside of ambition in a moment, but it's fair to say at the outset that ambition is destructive more often than not. The Bible speaks quite a bit about the dangers of ambition and its attendant temptations—the desire for power and money, and the need to be served rather than to serve. There are at least three instances where ambition is a danger which followers must avoid:

1. When it turns into a desire for power

The curious and troubling story of Simon Magus is told in Acts 8. Simon was a popular and well-known sorcerer in Samaria, known to the people by the somewhat lofty title, "the great power of God" (8:10, KJV). In these early days of the church the gospel was spreading rapidly and Philip's evangelistic message in Samaria had resulted in the conversion of many.

Amazingly, Simon Magus was one of those who believed and was baptized; he even began to follow Philip around, impressed by the apostle's own signs and wonders.

Peter and John soon came to join Philip in Samaria and as the apostles laid hands on the new Christians, they received a powerful filling of the Holy Spirit.

This show of power was too much for Simon, who burst out enthusiastically, "Give me also this ability so that everyone on whom I lay my hands may receive the Holy Spirit" (8:19).

Had the narrative ended here, we might have been content to point to Simon's outburst as the excessive enthusiasm of a new Christian who needed seasoning and spiritual maturity. But Peter's response was scathing, surprising in its intensity.

> Peter answered: "May your money perish with you, because you thought you could buy the gift of God with money! You have no part or share in this ministry, because your heart is not right before God. Repent of this wickedness and pray to the Lord. Perhaps he will forgive you for having such a thought in your heart. For I see that you are full of bitterness and captive to sin." (8:20-23)

Peter diagnosed the root of Simon's ambition for spiritual power as bitterness and captivity to sin. Perhaps he had resentment (hidden even from himself) at the fact that the apostles' signs and wonders had ended his own profitable magic show in Samaria. Whatever the cause, his desire to possess spiritual power was corrupt and destructive.

Power of any kind is a dangerous and addictive drug. In a very real sense, the heart of sin is the desire to be the sole source of power in our worlds, to be our own god and to determine and shape our own destiny. Conversion comes when we give up our pretensions to power and submit to God, the gracious, all-powerful One.

The heart of sin is the desire to be the sole source of power in our worlds.

Even after conversion, though, our latent thirst to control ourselves, our associates and our environment can be a dangerous source of mischief and evil in our lives. Bosses who must have power demoralize subordinates. Pastors who must play God taint their followers' views of the real, gracious God who uses His power only for good. Parents who exert excessive control over their families raise uncreative, lifeless and often deeply rebellious children.

Perhaps most dangerous of all is the ambition to be thought of as spiritually powerful. Ambition for reputation is a subtle yet deadly poison. Dallas Willard goes so far as to say that, along with the desire to accumulate wealth, the "desire to have the approval of others, especially for being devout" is one of the two main things that can hinder a life of responsiveness to and communion with God.[1]

In fact, this desire to be *seen* as spiritually powerful may have been just as potent and destructive a force for Simon Magus as was his desire to *possess* spiritual power. After all, he was a man of considerable reputation and was respected greatly by the townspeople. Reputation can be a hard thing to let go, and ambition for reputation can become a consuming quest, distracting us from the quiet, more important pursuits of building godly character and intimacy with the Father.

2. When it masks greed

Ambition for money was the downfall of Gehazi, the servant of the prophet Elisha. His story is found in Second Kings, chapter 5.

God, through Elisha, had miraculously healed Naaman, a military general, of leprosy. In return, Naaman had offered to lavish gifts on Elisha, but the prophet refused. Gehazi, on the other hand, saw an opportunity too good to waste. So he chased down Naaman's caravan and concocted a story about Elisha needing silver and clothing to give to two other prophets. It was a brazen, if unimaginative, scam; Gehazi hid the gifts to keep them for himself.

It's tough to fool a prophet, though, and Elisha knew what Gehazi had done. Gehazi compounded his treachery by lying to Elisha, and his punishment was a severe case of the same disease which Naaman had suffered, a punishment made more serious by the fact that the disease would affect not only Gehazi but his descendants.

The desire to make ourselves secure by stockpiling material things is identified by Willard as the other deadly curse on spiritual life. The allure of wealth and the security it promises to bring are no strangers to the pages of the Bible; various parts of Scripture contain multiple warnings about the seductive and destructive nature of materialism.

Greed is so deadly because it represents a lust to find security, meaning and significance apart from Christ. In our culture, possessing material things is an effective anesthetic to the sense of need we were meant to feel—a holy hunger and thirst for God.

Once greed has set into our lives, we are no longer able to think and reason sharply or to hear God clearly. Another god has first place and it is a god who will tolerate no rivals. "You cannot serve God and things," Jesus said (see Matthew 6:24). We have to choose one or the other.

Those of us who follow need to examine our hearts carefully and look for evidence of greed, the desire for the false security that material possessions bring. Left unchanged, a greedy heart violates trust, loses sensitivity to God and ruins any chance at fruitful ministry. We remember Elisha, not Gehazi.

3. *When it results in rebellion against God-given authority*

To put it boldly, rebellion against legitimate authority never pays off, at least not over time. And rebellion against spiritual authority appointed by God has particularly destructive consequences. It is important for followers to give loyalty and support to legitimate leaders and to put aside the inevitable temptations to be self-determined and to try to manipulate things outside of the structures God has established.

John the apostle dealt curtly with a rebellious follower named Diotrephes "who loves to be first" and "will have nothing to do with us." Evidently, Diotrephes was using his position of influence to turn aside legitimate traveling teachers sent by the apostles to instruct the church. When some protested his heavy-handed actions, he made sure that they were excommunicated (3 John 1:9-10).

It seemed that John did not want to waste his breath on such a scoundrel. "Don't let this bad example influence you," he writes. "Follow only what is good. Remember that those who do good prove that they are God's children, and those who do evil prove that they do not know God" (1:11, author's paraphrase).

Rebellion against legitimate spiritual authority, which always involves a desire for power or "loving to be the leader," is evil. Working with legitimate authority and following what is good is characteristic of God's children. This is John's spare, clear teaching.

John's concern over Diotrephes extended beyond his rebellious attitude, however. What was most troubling about this power-hungry man was his dictatorial approach to his own exercise of authority. He seems to have become the sole arbiter of who may or may not be part of the church. There is no place for authoritarianism in the church or among Christians in any context. Jesus' words in Mark 10, which we will examine in a moment, make this clear.

The greatest gift a follower can give to a leader is principled loyalty.

However, God gives to some the spiritual gift of leadership (Romans 12:8) and this gifting, combined with spiritual discipline, wisdom and maturity, confers a measure of spiritual authority that followers ought to respect. When such a person is in an official position of authority or leadership, this is simply a visible sign of an already-present spiritual reality.

The greatest gift a follower can give to a leader is principled loyalty. This is not blind loyalty, which disregards evident signs of ethical or spiritual wrongdoing on the part of the leader. But, in the absence of clear signs of wrongdoing, a follower owes to the leader loyalty, support and the benefit of the doubt.

Such principled loyalty is almost impossible to give if the follower believes that he ought to be in the leadership position. Over time, this belief, if nurtured and harbored, will corrode trust, contentment and joy in partnership. The consequences of this for the organization, the leader and, not least, the follower's own heart, are serious. Unchecked ambition that turns into rebellion destroys friendships, demeans ministries in the public eye, hamstrings businesses, splits families and creates a chain of spiritually explosive reactions with consequences that may last for years and even generations.

Learning the discipline of submission—to God and to those whom God has appointed to leadership—is a major component of becoming an effective follower and is an absolute prerequisite to effective leadership. Richard Foster writes wisely and well: "There is a power that comes through spiritual gifts and there is a power that comes through spiritual positioning. The two work in unison. Submission gives us spiritual positioning under the leadership of Christ. Submission is power because it places us in a position in which we can receive from others."[2]

There is a paradox here, as so much of following Jesus is paradoxical. The hard discipline of submission, which in our culture is equated with weakness, actually puts us in a position of strength where God's power and gifts can flow unchecked into our lives.

The antidote for rebellious ambition is basic but effective. First, acknowledge the sin, confess it to God and ask for forgiveness. Second, determine to act with integrity, faithfulness and loyalty toward the one you are following. Third, ask one or two friends who understand the spiritual dynamics involved and will hold you accountable to follow well and to check the ambition in your heart.

The hard discipline of submission actually puts us in a position of strength where God's power and gifts can flow unchecked into our lives.

A common thread in each of these ambition temptations is wasted energy. It just takes too much time, thought and effort to work for power or the reputation for power, to acquire material things and/or to mount a rebellion. It is so much more restful, energizing and fulfilling to channel all of our energies into good things like serving, faithfulness, prayer, love, good works and intentional, creative followership.

When Ambition Is from God

Not all ambition is evil, of course. There is ambition sent by God to spur us on to greater ministry and deeper growth in Christ. Let's look at a few examples.

The call to spiritual leadership

"If anyone sets his heart on being an overseer [elder]," wrote Paul to Timothy, "he desires a noble task" (1 Timothy 3:1). Paul then goes on to describe the qualities and characteristics of an effective elder.

What is significant about Paul's words is that he assumes that some will have an ambition—a heart's desire—to hold the position of elder. Not only is this appropriate, but it is expected. Aspiration to spiritual leadership, when it is the result of a genuine call, is a positive thing.

Merely desiring leadership, however, does *not* confer a call. The New Testament lists several confirmations of a calling to leadership—the primary one being a demonstration of the character qualities described in First Timothy and elsewhere. Another is the external call of the church to leadership.

Ambition alone is not adequate for leadership, but it is fairly rare that one is called to leadership without feeling a desire to lead. This may appear to run counter to the important truth that leaders must be servants. We are tempted to think that leaders are called "kicking and screaming" into leadership, resisting all the way, always preferring to take a backseat.

The fact is that this is a notion of false piety. It ignores the fact that leadership is a spiritual gift and that the teaching of the Bible is that we are most energized and alive when we are functioning in our giftedness to build up the body of Christ. And it ignores Paul's assumption in this passage that elder candidates will aspire to the position.

Those who hold to the idea of being called "kicking and screaming" into leadership often use Moses in front of the burning bush as an example. They fail to note that Moses' resistence to the call made God angry (Exodus 4:13-14).

Leaders serve by leading and servants lead by serving. The best, most called leaders want to lead, but are deeply aware that their calling is from God, that they are inadequate to lead if left to their own devices. They also know that they need the support and accountability of other leaders and followers to lead well.

The ambition to be used by God

The fact that ambition to be an elder is approved by Paul is an indication that not all ambition is bad. Christ-followers who understand the rich, good plan of God for His world and who are sensitive to the times in which we live will be full of ambition to have their lives count for God.

If we are ambitious to be used by God, we will long for our hearts to be open and receptive to God and others, and we will long for the coming of the reign and rule of God to be realized in the lives of more and more people and for us to play a part in that. We will trust God that He can take our own inadequacies, fears and shortcomings and use us to advance His purposes in the lives of others in startling, deeply transforming ways.

There is nothing wrong with this kind of ambition. In fact, we should cherish and nurture it.

The ambition to be a part of something bigger than we are

One of the results of spiritual maturity is that God gives us a picture of His heart and His actions that are far bigger than our individual concerns. Seasoned Christ-followers are characterized by their "big picture" mentality. Their hearts are tuned to what God is doing in the lives of those around them, in their community and across the globe.

This big picture mentality is nothing less than vision, the key asset of leaders. When a vision which has been given by God encounters a receptive leader's heart and touches human need, the resulting energy is remarkable in its effectiveness and depth. We should have a strong ambition to be part of something like this.

Endnotes

1. Dallas Willard, *The Divine Conspiracy* (San Francisco: Harper-Collins, 1998), p. 188.
2. Richard Foster, *Money, Sex, and Power* (San Francisco: Harper and Row, 1985), pp. 205-206.

Part Two

Qualities of a Faithful Follower

Chapter

3

The Follower as a Servant

Quick—what images come to your mind when you hear the word "servant"?

If you're like most of us, the images are none too glamourous or even attractive. Degrading images from the United States' shameful history of slavery may come to mind, perhaps fueled by scenes from Hollywood.

Whatever images come to mind, the accompanying adjectives are likely to run along these lines: downtrodden, hard-working, unappreciated, captive, put upon, disrespected. All other things being equal, not many of us want to be servants. Who wants a role that implies dishonor and low esteem?

The Bible has a way of creeping up on our preferences and biases and eating them alive. So it is with our desire to lead rather than to follow, to be served rather than to serve. The heroes of the Bible, most notably Jesus Himself, identified themselves and were identified by others as servants. In the Bible, "servant" is, as often as not, a term of honor, not disgrace.

Paul, the key leader in the early church, delighted to describe himself as a servant. He was a man sold out to Christ as his bond-servant (*doulos*), a term that actually denotes "slave" as much as "servant" (Romans 1:1, Philippians 1:1, Titus 1:1). Similarly, he views himself as Christ's personal servant (*diakonos*) (1 Corinthians 3:5; 2 Corinthians 11:23). In an extraordinary juxtaposition, Paul links his own task as an apostle with that as a servant to people: "For we do not preach ourselves, but Jesus Christ as Lord, and ourselves as your servants for Jesus' sake" (2 Corinthians 4:5).

Of all the images the Bible uses to describe followership, none is more powerful, rich or relevant than servanthood.

Of all the images the Bible uses to describe followership, none is more powerful, rich or relevant than servanthood. The title of servant is given special dignity because it is applied to the coming Messiah in the Old Testament (e.g., Isaiah 42:1-4; 52:13-53:12) and owned by Jesus in the New Testament (Mark 10:45,

John 13:12-16). Of all the servants in the Bible, Jesus stands alone as the ultimate model.

The Character of a Servant

Isaiah 42 describes the Servant of the Lord, an Old Testament figure later identified with Jesus:

> Here is my servant, whom I uphold,
> my chosen one in whom I delight;
> I will put my Spirit on him
> and he will bring justice to the nations.
> He will not shout or cry out,
> or raise his voice in the streets.
> A bruised reed he will not break,
> and a smoldering wick he will not snuff out.
> In faithfulness he will bring forth justice;
> he will not falter or be discouraged
> till he establishes justice on earth.
> In his law the islands will put their hope.
> (42:1-4)

A servant is a *chosen one,* selected for this task by God, who delights in His follower. A servant moves through life from the secure base of this identity as a chosen one. The service he or she performs is a response to being loved by God, not a desperate attempt to earn the Father's approval. Other things that we learn about servanthood from this passage are:

- A servant depends on the *Holy Spirit* for life, depth and power.
- A servant *does not draw attention to himself* and is *merciful.*
- A servant has a *tenacity of spirit*—a faithfulness that does not falter or remain discouraged.

Far from a mindless drone, the servant in Isaiah 42 is a picture of strength, resilience and passion, yet meekly submitted to the will of the Father by the power of the Spirit. An iron fist in a velvet glove.

Jesus: the Servant of the Lord in flesh and bone

On the night before His death, Jesus makes the extraordinary gesture of washing the grimy feet of His disciples, a task normally reserved for the most humble of household help.

After He acted out the role of a servant, Jesus drove His lesson into the hearts of His disciples:

> "Do you understand what I have done for you?" he asked them. "You call me 'Teacher' and 'Lord,' and rightly so, for that is what I am. Now that I, your Lord and Teacher, have washed your feet, you also should wash one another's feet. I have set you an example that you should do as I have done for you. I tell you the truth, no servant is greater than his master, nor is a messenger greater than the one who sent him. Now that

> you know these things, you will be blessed if you do them." (John 13:12b-17)

Jesus' point is clear. He is the ultimate servant and His disciples are called to emulate Him. This means that they will mimic Him by being servants as well. Rarely if ever was Jesus so clear to say that He was setting an example for His followers. But He wants there to be no mistake. He is a servant and His followers must be servants as well.

Earlier in His life, Jesus had laid out His mission statement in plain view. "For even the Son of Man did not come to be served, but to serve, and to give his life as a ransom for many" (Mark 10:45). Servanthood is at the heart of Jesus' identity and must be at the heart of our identity as well.

Another time, Jesus borrowed from the less flattering contemporary definition of a servant when He said to His disciples: "I no longer call you servants, because a servant does not know his master's business. Instead, I have called you friends, for everything that I learned from my Father I have made known to you" (John 15:15). Many think of servants as out of the loop, maybe even less than people. Jesus redefines the concept of servanthood to mean those who know the Father's heart and serve the Father's purposes.

In light of what Jesus said and did, we can add to our description of a servant's character:

- A servant is *willing to downsize his reputation* to serve others and won't shy away from demeaning tasks.
- A servant *sees servanthood as at the core of his identity*. Servanthood is a large part of a follower's life mission statement.
- A servant *knows the blessing of servanthood.* This is the deep, secure sense of being who God wants us to be and the joy that comes from knowing that our own character is growing more and more to resemble Jesus'.
- And, finally, a servant *is a friend of Jesus,* one who knows the Lord's heart and is growing in his understanding of God's purposes and values.

> Jesus redefines the concept of servanthood to mean those who know the Father's heart and serve the Father's purposes.

It should be clear that servanthood does not imply an abdication of leadership or responsibility. Servants are leaders and leaders are servants, as are followers. And servanthood does not involve giving up one's personhood and identity. On the contrary, we come to know who we are most fundamentally—the chosen ones in whom God delights—only when we give ourselves to serve God and others. The way of blessing is not self-promotion and expecting that I will be served, but through giving myself to others as a servant.

What Does a Servant Do?

Most of us who live in North America have no first-hand experience of servanthood. We have neither been servants ourselves nor had servants of our own. By contrast, the earliest readers of the Bible lived in a culture where servanthood was common; the metaphor of spiritual servanthood made sense to them. We are several steps removed. While we may accept the biblical pattern of servanthood and truly want to be servants, we don't always know how that plays out in practical terms. What does a servant look like? What does a servant do?

Ted Engstrom and Donald Dayton list nine qualities of followers which revolve around the theme of servanthood.[1] Together, they are a fine basic introduction to the nuts and bolts of a life of servanthood.

- *Commitment*. First to the leader, then to our colleagues and then to our organization.
- *Understanding*. We understand our task, those we work with and the context in which we serve.
- *Loyalty*. We are committed to the reputation of our leader and will represent him or her loyally and accurately.

- *Communication.* We provide the honest feedback and complete information our leader needs to do his or her job, even if the truth reflects badly on us.
- *Competence.* If we can't do the job, we serve the organization and its leaders by admitting so, choosing to risk our own reputation than to harm the mission of the organization.
- *Promise-Keeping.* We are straightforward about what we can and can't do and always honor our commitments.
- *Participation.* We subordinate our own desires, ambitions and even some needs to the mission and our colleagues and leaders. We are team players rather than free agents.
- *Getting Along.* We are vulnerable to others and committed to them as people, not just as cogs in a machine.
- *Sacrifice.* We are willing to pay any legitimate price for the leader, the mission and the organization. A legitimate price is one which does not cause us to violate biblical principles for conduct and ethics. If we want to be effective followers, we have to reckon with the fact that the price will, at times, be quite high.

A key decision for the early church illustrates the importance of servanthood in organizational leadership. As the church grew, the leaders were being stretched to the limit to meet the needs of all the people. Their primary work was spiritual leadership—activities such as teaching the Word and prayer. However, the practical demands and physical needs of the people were a distraction to them. Predictably, a conflict arose because some of the people were feeling neglected (an inevitable occurrence when leaders are unfocused). In this case, the distribution of food to economically dependent widows was the point of contention.

The task may not be glamorous,
but the calling of a servant is a high one.

In response, the apostles arranged to have seven men chosen who were "known to be full of the Spirit and wisdom" (Acts 6:3). The seven were selected, ordained and commissioned. These seven were the earliest "deacons" (*diakonos*), men given the specific task, explicit even in their title, of being servants.

But to be a servant was not a demeaning task. Servanthood is viewed as a noble calling, requiring wisdom and the fullness of the Spirit; the first deacons were carefully selected and worthy of ordination and commissioning. The task may not be glamorous, but the calling of a servant is a high one.

A leader will be out front, while a follower may be behind the scenes, but this in no way diminishes the importance of the follower/servant role.

Two Servants' Stories

I want to tell you the stories of two servants. One is my friend and former colleague, Tom Kakadelis, who is the director of congregational life and pastoral care for a church where I served. Tom has tremendous leadership gifts, the ability to connect instantly with people and a warm and engaging personality. He can "work a room" better than any political candidate I know!

Tom also has the heart of a servant. When there is an immediate physical need, Tom is the first to meet it—whether it's opening a door or pulling up another chair to the table. Tom has particular gifts and interests in the area of conflict resolution and mediation, and he has the heart of a servant for helping people work through tense relational issues. He and I traveled across the country once for a very difficult and painful crisis intervention, and I saw him care for all the parties involved with the firm, loving, patient and wise hand of a battle-tested servant.

Most of all, I remember a conversation I had with Tom in which he said, "The only way I know to influence people is to love and serve them. Everything else is just politics." Tom models the heart of a servant in his role as a pastor and the people he cares for are nudged closer to Christ because of it.

Then there is the story Leighton Ford tells about Helen Roseveare, an Irish medical missionary to Zaire.

She was the only doctor at a large, chaotic, under-equipped hospital and her position was off the charts in terms of stress and intensity. At one point, her irritation began to be obvious to those around her.

Her gentle African pastor came to the hospital one Friday afternoon and insisted that Helen come to his home for a weekend retreat. She prayed all of Saturday and most of Sunday, but she did not sense that her spirit was being restored.

Sunday evening she went to see her pastor as his family was cooking its evening meal outside. She confessed her struggles to pray and asked for his help.

"Helen, may I tell you what's the matter?" he asked. She nodded.

The pastor stood up and with his bare toe drew a long, straight line in the dust.

"That is the problem. There is too much *I,* too much *Helen,* in what you are doing."

Then he went on, "I have noticed you in the hospital. A number of times during the day you will take a brief break and ask for a cup of hot coffee. You hold that cup of coffee in both of your hands while it cools off, and then you drink it."

Again he took his big toe, and this time he drew another line across the first one.

"I want you to do this," he said kindly. "Every time you stand cooling that cup of coffee, why don't you say in your heart, 'Lord cross out the *I,* cross out the *I.*' "[2]

This is the most important thing.

Endnotes

1. Quoted in Eugene Habecker, *Rediscovering the Soul of Leadership* (Wheaton, IL: Victor Books, 1996), pp. 115-117.
2. Leighton Ford, *Transforming Leadership* (Downers Grove, IL: InterVarsity, 1991), pp. 158-159.

Chapter

4

The Follower's Personal Life

Effective followers live with a sense of urgency. They are caught up in a mission larger than themselves, part of a team to whom they are personally and professionally committed, and willing to expend large amounts of time, energy and passion to accomplish the mission to which God has called them. All of this makes for a very full, rich and exciting life. It can also make for a train wreck.

Followers need to insure that their lives are balanced between relationship and solitude, task and reflection, exertion and rest, being and doing.

The temptation to live an unbalanced life is particularly acute for those in professional ministry, but the reality of our postmodern world with its rapidly shifting rules and roles is that all of our lives can become chaotic if we don't operate out of a quiet center. We are called to play so many roles—employee and employer, roommate, boyfriend or girlfriend, parent or child, leader or follower. Unless we arrange the details of our lives in such a way that we move through life with purpose and calm direction, we can lose our effectiveness as followers and even harm ourselves and those around us.

It's All about Relationship

The distinguishing aspect of the Christian faith is that it is centered in a relationship with a perfectly relational God. Our faith does not involve primarily assent to propositions, though the gospel has propositional content. It is not adherence to a philosophy, though it is a worthy endeavor to attempt to forge a Christian worldview. At its heart, to be a Christ-follower is to be in the process of pursuing a relationship with the God who is there, who is real and who pursues us with His whole heart.

It follows that the most important aspect of our lives will be the relationships which God has given us. A balanced personal life will be one in which our key relationships are healthy, growing and prioritized. A balanced life springs from balanced relationships.

Relationship with God

The primary relationship for Christ-followers, obviously, is their relationship with God. We follow human leaders well to the extent that we are following God well; there is an organic connection between our inner life and our outer life. A healthy relationship with God will be Trinitarian—it will involve our interaction with all three Persons of the one God.

The distinguishing aspect of the Christian faith is that it is centered in a relationship with a perfectly relational God.

A follower will be a *willing servant of God the Father,* who seeks to submit every ambition, motivation and decision to God for examination, correction and transformation. Effective followers are committed to living transparent lives before God, trusting the Father with their heart. When leaders looks at their followers, they should see a life that shows signs of intimacy with a loving Father who gives security, joy and peace. Followers operate from the basis of these gifts of the Father and do not expect the leader or the job to meet these needs in their lives.

To borrow a phrase popularized by Willow Creek Community Church, an effective follower of people must first be a fully devoted follower of Jesus Christ. A follower will see more and more of his character *conformed to the character of Christ*. If we are living out of a center of a growing relationship with Christ, our life will look more and more like His. Jesus was submissive to the will of His Father, yet courageous in the face of temptation to sell out His mission or to compromise His character. Any worthy leader will love and cherish a follower with qualities like these.

The life of an effective follower will also be characterized by an *openness to and dependence on the Holy Spirit*. The life of a Christ-follower is a life lived in the Spirit, sensitive to His leadings and promptings, responsive to His correction, hungry and thirsty for His comfort and absolutely dependent on His power. An effective follower has learned how to hear and respond to the voice of the Spirit and how to make decisions and set priorities after seeking the Spirit's counsel.

Discipline leads to freedom

A rich, deep tradition in the church for those who seek a growing relationship with the Father is the way of the spiritual disciplines. The spiritual disciplines are those practices which nurture our life in the Spirit and make room for God to transform our hearts to be like Jesus' heart. There are several disciplines which are of particular importance for the follower.

The disciplines of *prayer* and *Scripture* are primary. The Bible tells us who God is and how He deals with us; it tells the Story which intersects our own stories, calling them into question and demanding decision. Prayer is the primary arena where our relationship with God is forged and matured. A life of ministry, a life of followership, self-control and dedication flows best from a deepening life of prayer in which the intercessor draws near to God's heart and learns to see life and people with the Father's eyes.

It sounds harsh, but it is true: many Christians don't read the Bible much and they pray even less. This is not meant to induce guilt—virtually all Christ-followers already feel some measure of guilt about their devotional lives—but rather to offer a reality check and to allow the Spirit room to tempt us with His sweetness.

Prayer is the primary arena where our relationship with God is forged and matured.

There are many distractions in our lives and many external props which make it possible for us to feel that we are managing our own lives just fine. And we live in a culture which tells us that externals—bigness, loudness, richness and impressiveness—are what matter most. All of this conspires to make it hard for us to hear God and, frankly, difficult for us to develop an appetite for Him.

But we will not follow God or others well or know God intimately unless we are willing to pay the price of pursuing a relationship with Him. The very disciplines which can feel like a heavy burden actually lead to freedom and joy, as we are primed spiritually to see what God is doing and join Him in it. Having unstopped ears to hear the gentle nudgings of the Spirit will lead us to make decisions and take courses of action that lead to rich reward and fruit.

In addition to the disciplines of prayer and Scripture, the disciplines of *solitude*, *simplicity* and *fasting* are important for followers. A follower, in partnership with leaders, is obligated to listen for God's vision. Solitude helps to create the quiet places where God can whisper His vision in our ears. Solitude—retreat from a noisy chaotic world—gives God room to deal with our hearts in depth, to teach us and give us His perspective, and most of all to get our attention so that He can tell us how much He loves us. It is hard and intense work to be a good follower. The regular discipline of solitude allows for the constant reexamination of priorities and motivations that may come between us and following well.

Simplicity is a supremely countercultural discipline which touches all areas of our lives—from the things we own to the schedules we keep to the relationships we maintain. The discipline of simplicity leads us to discern the core things to which God has called us and to see clearly what we actually need as opposed to what we merely think we want. Best of all for the follower, a life of material, emotional and spiritual simplicity allows us to move lightly through life, having our minds filled with God's Word and our lives unencumbered by distractions.

Fasting is closely related to simplicity in that it involves a renunciation of what we think we need so that God can give us what we truly need. Fasting is remarkably important for leaders because a key product of fasting is clarity of thought to receive God's vision. But followers need to fast too, because fasting surfaces our toughest indwelling sins and motivations, helps us to see as God sees, changes us permanently and mysteriously releases power in the unseen parts of creation (Isaiah 58).

Resisting Temptation

Followership was at the core of Jesus' mission while He was on earth. Jesus' commitment to follow His Father's leading regardless of the personal cost was tested repeatedly during the course of His time here. His resolve to follow well was never more tested than at the very beginning of His public ministry when He met the Tempter himself in the wilderness (Matthew 4:1-11, Mark 1:12-13, Luke 4:1-13).

Jesus' wilderness encounter with Satan followed right on the heels of His baptism by John. This was a moment of supreme affirmation for Jesus. The Father endorsed—audibly—the identity, life and ministry of Jesus. Nothing could have encouraged Jesus more than the endorsement and blessing of His Father.

Immediately after this emotional and spiritual high point, Jesus was led by the Spirit into the wilderness to face the most agonizing and grueling experience of His life, second to the events surrounding His death. The temptations which Jesus faced are a sort of pattern for the temptations we will face, and they have particular relevance for us as we think through what it means to follow well.

The temptation to exert power

Jesus had gone without food for forty days and was, understandably, hungry. Satan's first temptation was for Jesus to use His power to turn stones into bread. Such an act was well within the scope of Jesus' power and would have met an immediate and pressing need.

Jesus responded by rejecting the temptation outright and quoting Scripture, a pattern He followed for all three temptations. "Food is not the most important thing for life," Jesus said in effect. "Hearing and obeying God is even more primary" (see Matthew 4:4).

Jesus' temptation was to use the legitimate power He had at His disposal to serve illegitimate ends, ends outside of God's will for His life. To reject the temptation would be to reject meeting His own needs for nourishment and strength and to embrace the way of suffering and discipline and submission the Father intended for Him to follow.

Power is both subtle and seductive, especially where followers are concerned. The power threat is obvious for leaders; to be a leader is to possess, in some degree, the ability to acquire and use power. The power temptation is less obvious, but just as real for followers.

Followers are often at the center of the details of an organization, and so have enormous influence. Followers may have the ear of the leader and find themselves able to influence the organization through their advice and counsel. Followers often know where the bodies are buried and where the resources are hidden. An effective follower will find that he has at his disposal reservoirs of power in the form of influence, access and resources.

This is all well and good. But it may also be deadly. The consistent theme of the Bible is that power is not a neutral force. All other things being equal, power usually ends up corrupting the one who possesses it. Power unchecked, which means power not in submission to God's purposes, tends to cloud the perspective and taint the heart of most leaders and followers.

We as followers must be on our guard to prevent the temptation of power from sucking us into its trap.

An effective follower understands the dangers and temptations associated with power and has resolved to avoid power wherever possible and, when it must be held, to wield power lightly. This means that a follower will never use information, resources or influence to manipulate a leader or those around a leader or the constituency of the organization he serves. It means that a follower will often choose not to use information or resources that could be used to advance personal interests or lead to personal gain.

For Jesus, the temptation to use His power in inappropriate ways was a real temptation which, to all appearances, could have been justified. If our Lord could be tempted by the seduction of power, we as followers must be on our guard to prevent the temptation of power from sucking us into its trap.

The temptation to place demands on God

Next, Satan took Jesus to the highest point of the temple in Jerusalem and challenged Him to jump off and trust God to send angels to protect Him. Jesus responded by refusing to test God.

To test God is to demand that He act in a way that we determine to be best. To test God is to demand that He prove that He is good or powerful or faithful by passing tests we create for Him. We test God when we demand that He work in our lives to bring about the things we think we must have.

What is most dangerous about testing God is that we are, in effect, putting ourselves in His place. When we make demands of God we are assuming that we know best how He ought to conduct Himself. We are also assuming that we know what we need. Followers who have gifts and ambition and vision will often believe that they know what is best for their organization. They often believe that they know what is best for their own development and advancement within the organization.

Our temptation is to assume that our own understanding of what we and our organizations need meshes with God's point of view. The temptation takes root when we attach our sense of God's nearness and pleasure with external results and when we begin to manipulate people and circumstances to bring these results about.

The temptation to avoid suffering

Finally, Satan took Jesus to the top of a high mountain and offered Him unlimited earthly power and glory if Jesus would declare His allegiance to Satan. Presumably, this would have meant that Jesus would avoid the shame and suffering of the cross.

Jesus' response was swift and decisive. He affirmed that God and God alone could be worshiped and He banished Satan from His presence.

The force of this last encounter is that worship belongs to God alone. But we shouldn't ignore the temptation attached—the temptation to avoid suffering by shortcutting Jesus' mission of suffering and dying for our sins. This must have been a serious temptation to Jesus, because He knew what was coming—a gruesome death.

But Jesus knew that the road to servanthood, the road of a faithful follower, runs through the place of suffering. No one has ever accomplished great things for God without experiencing a measure of the pain and rejection associated with refusing to bow to the gods of the age.

"Following has about it a willingness to accept the possibility of our own execution," writes Ted Engstrom. "It may be the execution of personal dreams and aspirations. It may be the execution of our own highly held opinions. It may be the offering up of our individualism for the cause of which we are a part. . . . We discover that being a good follower calls for sacrifice we never imagined."[1]

The road to servanthood runs through the place of suffering.

To follow well means to be willing to suffer by being misunderstood, rejected, devalued, ignored or put upon. Following is inglorious most of the time. All of the time it is hard work. Sometimes it will cost you your life.

Every follower involved in significant work will face each of these temptations, often multiple times—the temptation to exert power, the temptation to place demands on God and the temptation to avoid suffering. The way in which we respond to these temptations will be directly related to the quality and depth of our lives. This richness is a direct product of the time we have been willing to invest in paying the price for the spiritual disciplines which nurture and mature our walk with God.

Relationships with Others

There is a truth that is hard but necessary for American Christ-followers to accept. It is this: The Bible says very little about "me and Jesus" and a great deal about "us and Jesus." Christ came to call individuals together into a new community which would follow Him, not simply to call individuals to follow Him. If the Bible has a grand preoccupation, it is God's desire to bring people together in a new community centered on new life in Jesus Christ.

From beginning to end, the Bible is all about community—from Eden in Genesis, in which perfect community is shattered, to the New Jerusalem in Revelation and the amazing picture of perfect community restored. This is a tough thing to accept for many in our culture, which conditions us to make our own way as autonomous individuals. But the New Testament knows little of independence. Its emphasis is on an interdependent community, with all its members preeminently dependent on Christ.

Three key relationships

To have a balanced relational life, an effective follower needs several of each of these types of relationships: friends, partners and mentors.

Followers need *friends,* people with whom they connect and see life similarly. These are the people we socialize with, those we call on a difficult day; they should also be those who sharpen our focus on God. "Let us consider how we may spur one another on toward love and good deeds," said the writer of Hebrews (10:24); this is an apt description of rich friendships. Friends spend time helping each other, laughing and crying together, moving through all of the chaos of life with nurture and support.

An important aspect of friendship is personal accountability. At least a few friends need to have access to the dark, private corners of my life. They need to know my struggles and sins so that they can call me on the carpet when need be and remind me of God's incredible grace which can cleanse and transform me.

Followers also need *partners,* those who share a similar vision for their work or ministry. These are people who share a similar life mission and purpose. Partners may be within the follower's organization or without, but they share similar passion and direction. An important function of partners is vocational accountability—holding one another to standards of excellence and keeping one another focused on the mission and vision.

Every effective follower also has one or more *mentors,* individuals who are at least a few steps ahead on the journey and who can provide wisdom, perspective, spiritual guidance, correction and support. Certainly, followers who become effective leaders will do so, in part, because of the mentors God has given them to help navigate the waters of organization, vocation, professional development, heart development and spiritual formation. It would be particularly helpful for followers who want to grow in their followership to ask for help and feedback from effective followers who are a few years older.

The relationship with the leader

Part Three of this book focuses on the dynamic relationship between leaders and followers. For now, it is important to say that it is the responsibility of the follower to make sure that there are clear lines of communication, that trust is established and growing and that the leader can be assured of the dedication, loyalty and support of the follower. A good leader will take initiative to make sure that the leader-follower relationship is a mutually beneficial one. But a good follower will not wait around for the leader to act.

An authentic, growing, balanced inner life gives a follower a solid, centered base from which to live. The inner life lived transparently before God is where effective following begins. And it is this kind of life which provides the strength needed to avoid the pitfalls and fallacies common to followers, to which we turn next.

Endnote

1. Ted Engstrom, "Followership." *Christian Leadership Letter*, September, 1986, p. 3.

Chapter

5

Fallacies of Followers

As we explore the art of followership together, we'll spend a lot of time looking at what makes great followers, the behaviors and values that result in empowered followers and trusting leaders. But no discussion of the upside of followership is complete without taking into account the downside. What happens when followership goes bad?

In this chapter, we will take a look at some of the fallacies of followership, the traps which can fray or even destroy the fragile relationship between leader and follower.

Another image we might use is that of followership "sickness." When our bodies are sick, they feel as if they're in revolt against themselves. Something is present in our bodies that ought not to be there—perhaps a virus or bacteria of some kind—and the balance of our bodies is thrown off. Unless a cure is applied, there is the chance that the sickness can advance and shut the whole body down.

This is exactly what can happen with followership sickness. Unless it is diagnosed and treated quickly and effectively, it can kill relationships, churches, ministries and businesses. For this reason, we will also discuss some cures as we examine the several different strains of sickness, the fallacies of followership. The first step, however, to understanding any disease is to note the symptoms. Here are a few.

> Unless it is diagnosed and treated quickly and effectively, followership sickness can kill relationships, churches, ministries and businesses.

Unquestioning Conformity: The "Yes" Person

If there hadn't been a nameplate on her cubicle desk, you might never have known that Diane was there. Actually, she occupied an important position in the ministry as development director. She was responsible for networking and cultivating relationships to insure a steady and growing donor base. But none of her coworkers would have been able to name a single initiative she had introduced or creative idea she had implemented.

Diane's organization was led by Dr. Gordon, its seventy-something founder. A large man in build, he was larger in reputation and personality. He dominated the organization by his force of personality, commanding presence and seniority.

In recent years, a group of thirty-something executives had been hired and were beginning to shake things up a bit, which didn't always thrill Dr. Gordon.

The success of the organization had been built in part on Dr. Gordon's ability to raise large sums of money for its activities. For years, it had been tough to turn the doctor down. All he had to do was show up at a foundation or church, tell a few stories, hail old friends in his booming voice, lean over and look into the eyes of a grant committee chairperson, and the dollars came rolling in. There was never much follow-up with donors; there didn't need to be. Everyone trusted Dr. Gordon and the checks kept flowing in.

Until lately, that is. In the last fifteen years, the financial decision-makers in churches and foundations had become leaders from the Baby Boom generation. Many of them didn't know Dr. Gordon's past, they didn't like his occasionally overbearing style, and they were much less bound by institutional loyalty and tradition. Contributions had fallen off gradually, but had begun to take a noticeable decline in the last few years, as more members of Generation X assumed leadership in the churches and foundations. These leaders didn't care at all for Dr. Gordon's style and had no use for the practice of continuing to send checks "because we've always done it." The financial situation of the ministry was at a crisis point.

Dr. Gordon's younger executives had finally convinced their leader of the need for a full-time director of development. Diane's coming was widely heralded as the salvation of the organization. She was in her thirties and well-educated—just the person (it was assumed) to open a new era of prosperity and donor loyalty. Her supervisors knew there would be a few rough early tangles with Dr. Gordon, but once she weathered those, Diane would be able to move ahead.

The only problem was that she never tangled with the doctor and never moved ahead! Her early meetings with Dr. Gordon had not gone well as he assured her, "The way we've always done it will continue to work; just focus on the relationships I've built. I don't want to play around with any risky experiments. If we keep our long-time donor base happy, things will be all right."

Six months later, Diane sat in her office with nothing to show for her efforts. Dr. Gordon was happy with her compliance, but her other supervisors were frustrated. Worst of all, Diane felt as if she had made a compromise with her own convictions, though she did admire and respect Dr. Gordon. To Diane, submission to spiritual authority meant never challenging a leader on important issues.

Diane is a classic conformist. She goes along with the culture and traditions of an organization and, especially, with the most dominant leader. And she does this uncritically, for the most part.

On the outside, conformists can seem like valuable members of the team. They accept assignments without complaint, always trust their supervisors, never challenge decisions and never cause conflict.

But, as with other followership fallacies, the downside is greater that the upside. Conformists lack ideas and initiative, avoid conflict even when a course of action is unwise or dangerous, and lack the courage to take unpopular stands even when they are sure they are right. Conformists very rarely have credibility in the eyes of their colleagues.

Conformists are slow to ask critical questions and quick to acquiesce.

An organization of conformists can run quite well for a time, particularly if it is given dominant, visionary direction. But after a while the organization loses momentum, creativity and growth. There is also a good chance that the gifts and skills of the leaders will erode because they haven't been sharpened and challenged by others.

It may seem an unlikely comparison, but Adam is perhaps the archetypal conformist. After Eve made her fateful decision to eat the forbidden fruit, she gave some to Adam and "he ate it" (Genesis 3:6). Just like that!

Adam knew the terms and conditions God had placed on residency in the garden as well as he knew his own name. All was his and everything was permitted, except for the fruit from one tree. But when his wife offered him the contraband food, Adam went ahead and ate it, and we have no indication of even a hint of internal struggle.

When God confronted Adam and Eve about their rebellion, Adam's response was revealing: "The woman you put here with me—she gave me some fruit from the tree, and I ate it" (3:12).

Conformists go along with whatever way the prevailing wind is blowing, particularly if that wind is hot air blown by a determined or charismatic leader. Conformists are slow to ask critical questions and quick to acquiesce. If criticized for their inaction or their mindless compliance, they are quick to deflect blame to leaders. We are reminded of the legions of Nazi bureaucrats who carried out the most horrific crimes without question, all in the name of obedience and discipline. Their excuse? "I was just following orders."

While the stakes will be lower than that for us, it is still the case that conformist followers have the potential to damage or even destroy organizations by their lack of initiative. At the very least, followers who never question the process or respectfully challenge their leaders are depriving the organization of their gifts and their leaders of the opportunity to grow and learn.

The Cure for Conformity

The treatment for a conformist has two parts, both of which are essential for a complete cure.

First, a conformist has to *learn to ask good, critical questions.* A conformist's strength is that he trusts his leader. Good! But his weakness is that he assumes that his relationship with his leader is one-way. The best leader-follower relationships are mutual ones, where there is give and take, common respect and honoring of one another's gifts. A conformist has to begin to look at the challenges he and his leader face with new eyes. Assume for a moment that you were the one giving direction, not the leader. What would you do? What questions would you ask? What steps would you take?

A conformist has to acknowledge and deal with the fear of conflict and then learn how to engage in healthy disagreement.

If you can ask these kinds of questions and dialogue about them with your leader—always respectfully and always acknowledging the leader's role—you will serve your leader and become a more useful follower.

Second, a conformist has to *acknowledge and deal with the fear of conflict* and then learn how to engage in healthy disagreement. The adjective "healthy" is important here. There is a fine line between creative, fruitful disagreement and destructive conflict based on the desire to control, wield power or be vindicated. But since the conformist is tempted to avoid conflict altogether, he must concentrate on learning to engage in conflict that honors the other person and acknowledges appropriate roles, yet stretches the conformist to stand firm on matters of conviction.

A good guiding passage for a conformist is Paul's promise of what happens in our lives as we mature spiritually:

> Then we will no longer be like children, forever changing our minds about what we believe because someone has told us something different or because someone has cleverly lied to us and made the lie sound like the truth. Instead, we will hold to the truth in love, becoming more and more in every way like Christ. (Ephesians 4:14-15, NLT)

Alienated Cynicism: The Devil's Advocate

The opposite of the unquestioning conformist is the follower who challenges every opinion and directive of the leader. This type of follower almost unfailingly opposes the leadership regardless of the issue.

Ironically, devil's advocates usually start out as promising performers. They have potential because they have developed skills which conformists lack—critical and independent thinking, courage and initiative. But something goes wrong over time, so that a promising performer becomes an adversary to leadership.

Devil's advocates are typically cynical and sarcastic. They enjoy the image of a battle-scarred veteran, wise to the ways of the organization's world. They complain about bureaucracy, systems and structures. If their leadership is visionary and creative, devil's advocates accuse them of being power-hungry and too task-oriented. If the leaders are more cautious, devil's advocates accuse them of being stodgy and conservative. The only common denominator is complaint, with a healthy dose of feeling put upon and taken advantage of.

A devil's advocate can poison the hearts and minds of other employees, destroy his leader's effectiveness and damage his own reputation.

To be fair, there are usually legitimate sources for a cynic's resentment. Even the best organizations have employees with unmet expectations who have suffered broken promises. Over time, these incidents can create a climate of mistrust and wariness which fosters cynicism and caution. But a devil's advocate is unable to handle setbacks and disappointments that others are able to endure.

Over time, a devil's advocate can poison the hearts and minds of other employees, destroy his leader's effectiveness and damage his own reputation. Outsiders sense when an organization is full of devil's advocates. At the same time, one talkative devil's advocate can do tremendous public damage to an organization's credibility.

The Cure for Alienated Cynicism

The cure for a devil's advocate is not painless, but it is effective. It involves a reorientation of one's mind, a refocusing:

- from rights to responsibilities.
- from bitterness to forgiveness.
- from a critical spirit to one that seeks to understand.
- from the desire to be right to the desire to be faithful.

The good news for a devil's advocate is that he has some good things in place: initiative, independent thinking, courage. The even better news is that he has the opportunity to learn some of the deeper lessons of discipleship and spiritual authority: submission to godly leadership, trust, a servant's heart, speaking which builds up rather than tears down.

Mindless Coexistence: The Passive Sidekick

A cousin of the "yes" person is the passive sidekick—one who is more than willing to follow the leader's direction but unwilling to offer ideas and input or work above the bare minimum.

The leaders and colleagues of passive sidekicks often describe them as lazy and unmotivated. It's not that they refuse to do things; it's that they do no more than they have to, and there is never anything exemplary about their work. Their colleagues resent them because they only move when the boss gives orders and are unlikely to help out with a project unless they have a personal interest in it.

Followers who fall into the fallacy of mindless coexistence do not appear to harm the organization, at least on the surface. But over time, their lack of sacrifice, commitment to the team and willingness to pay the price to accomplish the organization's mission will hurt their own area of responsibility and create a demoralizing influence on others.

The Cure for Mindless Coexistence

The beginning of a cure for mindless coexistence is to ask a simple question: *Why am I here?* Why has God put me in this position, this job, this role, with these people, at this time, for this purpose? In other words, the cure for mindless coexistence is to engage the mind with questions that require thought, prayer and vision.

Once the answer has come, it will be difficult for a passive sidekick to continue in that role without directly choosing to disobey God. Here's why: God has given each of us a calling that is based on our temperament, personality, natural and spiritual gifts and His larger purposes. Our callings are different, but none of them are unimportant.

Next to coming to a relationship with God through Christ, nothing you will ever do is more important than identifying and living out your calling. To live out your calling requires great intensity. It takes single-minded purpose, sacrifice and devotion. It takes courageous action, deep thought and prayerful initiative. In other words, it takes everything that a passive sidekick fails to do.

The problem with passive sidekicks is that they haven't yet seen what God is up to in the world and what their role in that is. This is calling by definition. If they were to have a glimpse of the great purposes of God and the fact that God uses us to extend His purposes even with our insignificance, failings and weaknesses, they would be more than motivated to relish and embrace the role of a follower. They are not working for man, but for God—and this makes all the difference.

The problem with passive sidekicks is that they haven't yet seen what God is up to in the world and what their role in that is.

If you are a passive sidekick, ask God to give you a vision of His purposes and your role in that. Then renew the direction of your heart, mind and soul to get on the field and join His game!

Pragmatic Politics: The Ambitious Successor

The latter days of Boris Yeltsin's presidency of the Russian Republic were not pretty. As reports of the president's failing health spread, one could almost see his subordinates jockeying for position, influence and power. Every now and then, one of them would come out with an unauthorized pronouncement that the president was not doing well and would shortly resign.

Such announcements are typically followed by firings, resignations and Cabinet shake-ups. It must have been like walking a highwire to be a Yeltsin deputy with designs on greater things. You had a feeling that he would step down or die in office any day, so you knew it was important to preen, play to the press and shaft your rivals. On the other hand, there was life left in the old man yet and he seemed to enjoy lowering the boom on those who had a bit too much ambition for his taste.

The tension in being a Yeltsin deputy illustrates nicely what it's like to fall into the last followership fallacy we'll examine—the quagmire of pragmatic politics, playing the role of ambitious successor.

The ambitious successor is a follower who believes he has been called to greater things. At first, he is content to serve his leader and works hard, long and well, attracting the attention of others along the way.

But he wants to be more than a career follower, so he is soon looking for chances to distinguish himself above others, to curry favor with the right people in positions of power and to think about how he can advance in the organization.

Now there is nothing wrong with these things in themselves. It is not wrong to want to perform well, use one's gifts to the utmost and to leave a mark on the world. Ambition is not necessarily out of bounds even in the church. "If someone wants to be an elder," wrote Paul to Timothy, "he desires an honorable responsibility" (1 Timothy 3:1, NLT). Paul's implication is that it is not only permissible but proper to desire leadership.

But as we discussed in a previous chapter, there is a grave danger to ambition: It can be toxic in the lives of those who are not spiritually sharp and sensitive. Ambition is just a millimeter removed from a lust for pride and power. Ambition can also flow from a heart hungry for meaning and significance and determined to find those things apart from the approval of God.

Ambition can lead to every decision, interaction and relationship being filtered through the grid of this question: *Does this serve to meet my desire for advancement and enlarged influence?* In other words, unholy ambition at its heart is self-centered.

Ambition can become an idol in a heartbeat. An idol is anything in our lives that takes the place of God, consciously or unconsciously. Even good things can become idols when they capture our hearts and we begin to plan our lives around achieving or maintaining them. The Bible is loaded with dire warnings about the dangers of idolatry. These warnings are gracious because God knows how putting anything in His place will ultimately leave us miserable and unsatisfied.

The leader-follower relationship can become uniquely tainted by ambition when the issue of succession is relevant. It is part of a leader's responsibility to prepare the way for his successor; indeed, it is commonly held in the marketplace that succession planning is one of the most important priorities of the CEO. And it is fitting that a leader is concerned to mentor and develop protégés who may well follow him or her in leadership.

The leader-follower relationship can become uniquely tainted by ambition when the issue of succession is relevant.

But there are dangers here for both follower and leader. It is possible that the leader will try to control or manipulate the follower to maintain a sense of control over the organization. Once the leader has selected a successor, he may treat others unfairly or overlook flaws in the follower because his own decision is on the line. On the other hand, a leader can feel threatened by an heir apparent. It is not uncommon in business for a leader to sabotage the career of an employee who has been chosen to succeed him. In the church, the last several years have seen several high-profile ministries nearly implode when a retired leader, unable to let go of influence and power, set out deliberately to sabotage a handpicked successor.

The follower tapped for succession, on the other hand, may chafe under the bridle of the leader and may become impatient for his turn at leadership. This can result in a fractured relationship and bad decisions made in haste because the follower wanted to leave his mark and remind his colleagues that he will one day be in charge.

It is important that a board or other empowered leadership body monitor closely succession planning and execution to insure clear communication, orderly process and mutually agreed-upon expectations.

Whether or not succession is in mind, the danger of pragmatic political game-playing is all too real and will always distract followers from the mission of the organization and, worse, from the mission of every Christ-follower: to be a servant who considers others more important than himself.

The Cure for Pragmatic Politics

I know of no better way to put it than this: life is too short for political game-playing. The life of an ambitious successor takes a tremendous amount of energy to sustain, because he has to pay attention not only to his service, but to the impression his service is making on others and on how he matches up to potential rivals. Pragmatic politics requires time to discern the prevailing political winds and time to consider how to respond.

It's all just terribly silly—a waste of time and energy. In biblical terms, pragmatic politics represents bad stewardship: a squandering of responsibilities, time and gifts to pursue a selfish end.

A vision for God's calling is such a motivating thing that it makes political power games seem tasteless by comparison.

An ambitious successor doesn't know his purpose for living, and this is where we will find the key to the cure. Once an ambitious successor discerns, through prayer and counsel, the reason God made him, the particular mission for which he was created, all other priorities will be crowded out of the field of vision. A vision for God's calling is such a motivating thing that it makes political power games seem tasteless by comparison.

At his root, an ambitious successor doesn't know who he really is and, in his effort to define and claim an identity, he goes to almost any length to create himself. It is much better to respond in patience and willingness to the creating God has already done.

Enough about the potential fallacies of followers. Let's talk about what followers can do to serve with excellence.

Part Three

Followers and Leaders

Chapter

6

What a Leader Really Needs

Eli Black was one of the most gifted and feared businessmen of his generation. Charming and brilliant, vicious and cunning, Black was a complex man of many contradictions. He led the multimillion-dollar takeover of the American Fruit Company. And he jumped to his death from the forty-second floor of his office building.

Thomas McCann, one of Eli Black's top executives, described his former boss as a man who could make major decisions in a snap, fire those with whom he was displeased without hesitation, and skillfully practice the art of corporate politics and power games.

At a luncheon meeting with several other executives, a waiter brought a platter of cheese and crackers to the table. Black reached across the table, pulled the platter in front of himself and crossed his arms in front of the food, clearly marking his territory. As his hungry business partners salivated, Black began a long discussion about office building development in Latin America, ignoring the appetizer in front of him.

After many long minutes, Black selected a cracker, poised it on his fingertips, dug into the cheese with his knife and slowly spread cheese on the cracker. As he continued to lead the discussion, the cracker remained perfectly poised on his fingertips, drawing the rapt attention of the other men. After a great deal of time, Black suddenly deposited the cracker on Thomas McCann's plate, recrossed his arms in front of the platter and continued the discussion as if nothing had happened.

Eli Black knew how to play power games and manipulate the emotions of his followers. He was responsible for his actions and largely responsible for the succession of events which led to his lonely suicide.[1]

But what is striking about Thomas McCann's account is that Eli Black was never challenged by his followers. Given their full obedience but never their hearts, never called to account for his abuse of power, Eli Black was a bad leader served badly by his followers. And his story raises at least two questions for those of us who follow both great and not-so-great leaders: *How can followers who want to serve Christ also serve their leaders? And what do leaders really need from their followers?*

Effective followership is countercultural in its very essence. Followers are concerned with being servants first, with losing themselves in a larger cause and with mutual submission in love. Followers are not sheep, blindly led by omniscient and fault-free leaders. But neither are they consumer-oriented individualists, looking out for their interests and needs alone. Effective followers of Christ are concerned with meeting the needs of their leaders, even leaders who are not inclined to admit that they have needs.

Effective followers of Christ are concerned with meeting the needs of their leaders, even leaders who are not inclined to admit that they have needs.

Understanding and meeting a leader's needs takes practice, close attention and creativity. As a start, let's look at some of the most important needs held in common by leaders.

Love

The first question for followers who have a heart to serve their leaders is a stark one: *Do I love my leader, and do others know it by watching me?* Loving one's boss is not high on the priority list of most Americans, but it must be for followers of Christ. I don't mean the emotional experience of warm feelings. Even advanced

Christ-followers will struggle to feel warmly toward a cranky, arbitrary or power-hungry leader.

But the choice to love—to seek another's good above one's own—is not an option, but a requirement. It is difficult at times to love well. Love requires sacrifice, humility, a studied determination to put another first and constant reliance on the Holy Spirit. It has a cost. And that is the definition of discipleship.

The choice to love your leader—
to seek his good above your own—
is not an option, but a requirement.

Your Belief in Them

Leaders, even good ones, are a notoriously sensitive lot, as every follower can attest. Some leaders choose to cover up this sensitivity with bravado and a determined quest to appear confident in all situations, at all costs. Wise followers know the truth, though. "Leaders cannot maintain authority," writes leadership theorist John Gardner, "unless followers are prepared to believe in that authority. In a sense, leadership is conferred by followers."[2] A leader must have the confidence of his followers if he is to succeed over the long term.

Another key question for followers is: *Do I really believe in my leader, and do others know that?* If I can't trust my leader's heart or motives, then I need to consider having another leader. But if I do, at bottom, I need to act on that trust and to make sure that my leader and our colleagues know this.

It is difficult to overemphasize how important it is for a leader that his followers trust his heart and believe in his capabilities. The trust of followers can turn a mediocre leader into an effective one; a good leader can approach greatness with such a boost of confidence. Followers are able to *bless* their leaders—in the fullest, richest, most biblical sense of the term—by their confidence and joyful willingness to follow. In doing so, they bless themselves, because a confident leader is able to create a gracious environment within which followers can exercise their giftedness and creativity.

Your Support for Their Vision

Dean Smith, the legendary former basketball coach of the University of North Carolina, once offered this definition of coaching: *bringing a diverse group of individuals to a unity of purpose.* Throughout his long tenure in Chapel Hill, Smith's teams were characterized by a remarkable consistency in playing style, philosophy and success. Even his less-talented teams won repeatedly. Smith's bottom-line commitment to a common purpose served by all of the members of the team resulted in the most successful program in college basketball history.

Coach Smith's definition of coaching is a near-perfect description of leadership. Unity of purpose and mission is served by a willingness of diverse individuals to abandon themselves to the larger vision. The nearly impossible task of a leader in these relatively self-centered times is to create this kind of buy-in and mutual sacrifice.

The Christian leader and follower would add one element to Coach Smith's mix: The vision which unifies must be given by God and in accordance with Scripture. This is the element of authority which commands and beckons our followership.

If we are in a place of followership where we believe that the vision is from God and is in accordance with Scripture, we are to give our faithful loyalty and service. Normally, this vision will come through a leader who helps followers to hear from God and then articulates the common vision in a clear and compelling way.

If we are in a place of followership where the vision is from God and in accordance with Scripture, we are to give our faithful loyalty and service.

If this process has been played out, a follower really has no question about whether to follow or not—the decision has been made.

It is important, then, to make sure that we understand the vision of the leader prior to committing to serve an organization, whether as an employee or a volunteer. It is wise for us to ask probing, penetrating questions about both the content of the vision and the way in which the vision will be carried out prior to signing up.

When leaders and followers in an organization are united in vision and their constituency is committed to the way in which the vision is lived out, it is almost impossible to stop the success of the team.

Support for Other Team Members

Dissension in the ranks eats up a leader's time, cripples corporate vision and saps the organization's energy to carry out its mission. Church and ministry staffs seem particularly prone to dissension and infighting. Perhaps part of this is due to an idealistic expectation that those in ministry are supposed to be a special, more holy breed.

Whatever the reason, those who would be effective followers will avoid at all costs jealousy, backbiting and territorialism on ministry staffs or in the marketplace.

For a number of years, I was privileged to serve as part of a church staff team marked by collegiality and unity of spirit and of purpose. Even though we were a diverse group, from different backgrounds, different parts of the country and even different denominations, I can count on one hand the times we had unnecessary conflict.

The leader of the team was a man not given to pride, raw ambition or jealously. He set the pace for our team. But his staff helped him as well, by affirming in its practice the values of cooperation, mutual encouragement and the belief that the individual members of our organization are best served by the success of the whole. In such a climate, creativity and gifts flower. It was fun to come to work and to serve the Lord's people in such a place. I hope the organization I lead now is the same kind of place.

Effective followers should ask, *Am I making "every effort to keep the unity of the Spirit through the bond of peace" (Ephesians 4:3)? Am I creating ways to "spur [my colleagues] on toward love and good deeds" (Hebrews 10:24)?* If I am, then the chances are good that others are too and that my leader oversees a joyful, dedicated and successful team.

Your Integrity

As far as Bob was concerned, Ted was an ideal staff associate. Bob, a senior pastor, leaned heavily on Ted's expertise in his program area and on his advice and experience. Bob often drew Ted aside to help him think through issues and problems in his ministry, particularly in his relationships with several other staff members—relationships which had been under some strain due to a disagreement over budget priorities.

Ted was unfailingly upbeat and positive as he interacted with Bob, offering words of encouragement and support to his boss, and offering to help in any way he could. "You are the leader God has for this place," Ted assured Bob. "Eventually those guys will have to come around to the point of understanding that God has made you leader here and that their job is to follow. Either that, or they will have to move on."

What Bob didn't know was that Ted was offering the same encouragement to his staff colleagues. "Nothing against Bob," Ted would say to his coworkers, "but it's time for some fresh ideas and vision around here. And I think God has brought you guys here to offer that. Bob and the board are going to have to make a choice—either be open to change, or look to make a change at the top."

To act with integrity is to act from commitment to principle, even when that principle conflicts with self-interest.

Perhaps Ted believed that he was acting shrewdly, staying above the fray of a brewing conflict and positioning himself to win regardless of who came out on top. In fact, he was demonstrating a lack of integrity.

Integrity implies wholeness. A person of integrity is internally unified and consistent in all situations, regardless of external pressures and temptation. To act with integrity is to act from commitment to principle, even when that principle conflicts with self-interest.

In the Bible's language, to have integrity is to be "single-minded." David's prayer for his son Solomon was that he would have a "wholehearted devotion and . . . a willing mind"—that he would be a person of devotion and principle. And with good reason, for "the LORD searches every heart and understands every motive behind the thoughts" (1 Chronicles 28:9).

Integrity in one's personal conduct is one of the most precious gifts a follower can give a leader. A leader knows that a follower of integrity will speak honestly, even when the truth is not what the leader wants to hear. A leader knows that a follower of integrity will not shade a conversation to benefit himself, or misrepresent the leader's thoughts and intentions to make himself look better at the leader's expense.

Most importantly, a leader can count on such a follower's heart to move in obedience to God and in submission to God's purposes. With such followers, a leader can move with confidence and peace, even in the middle of challenging and dangerous situations.

Those of us who follow should examine our hearts carefully, praying that the Spirit of God will reveal to us our dark intentions or self-serving desires. These must be raised to the light, confessed and healed. We should ask ourselves, *Are my actions, words and motivations in this situation pure, above board and transparent to others?*

There is no stronger evidence for the reality of the Christian message than Christ-followers who move through life with integrity. All too often, we have failed this test corporately in our churches, workplaces and organizations. Organizations of integrity begin with leaders and followers of integrity. The stakes are high, not only for the success of our mission, but for our very credibility in the culture we seek to reach for Christ.

The Truth

Closely related to the issue of integrity is the issue of truthfulness. Ted's failure extended beyond his lack of integrity into the realm of truth-telling. An effective follower would have told both Pastor Bob and his fellow staff members the truth as he understood it. "Bob," he might have said, "it seems to me that you are not listening carefully enough to the other guys. Perhaps they are closer to the situation than you are and have a better sense of how our money should be spent." Or it might have been appropriate for him to confront his coworkers in this way: "Guys, I understand your concerns, but the fact is that Bob has been at this a whole lot longer than we have and has been through these sorts of questions before. It seems to me that your insistence on being right is pretty close to arrogance."

The truthfulness of followers, proved over time, will encourage leaders and give them confidence in those they must lead.

Giving out incomplete or misleading information in an effort to protect yourself, saying that things are fine when they are not or shading the truth to save someone's feelings may seem safe in the short term, but telling anything less than the truth is a disservice to everyone involved. It hampers the leader's ability to lead and your coworkers' ability to follow.

Followers should ask themselves, *Am I being tempted to shade the truth to make myself look better or to spare anyone's feelings? Am I committed to speaking the truth in love at all times?* The truthfulness of followers, proved over time, will encourage leaders and give them confidence in those they must lead.

Courage

It is easy to picture Barnabas as a happy-go-lucky, sentimental guy who was always smiling. A title like "Son of Encouragement" might lead us to visualize a big softy who was a pushover for driven "Type A" personalities. An examination of the historical record in Acts 15, however, paints a different picture.

On an earlier missionary journey, the young John Mark had become frightened or discouraged and left Paul and Barnabas to return home. For the results-oriented and mission-focused Paul, John Mark's failing disqualified him from future partnership. For the people-focused Barnabas, however, John Mark's struggles were a learning experience to be built on for future ministry. Barnabas wanted to give John Mark a second chance. Paul refused. Paul chose Silas as his new partner in ministry, while Barnabas chose to travel with John Mark, giving up the safety of working with a strong leader for the uncertainty of mentoring a novice with a spotty track record.

Effective followers demonstrate this kind of courage in the face of adversity. Barnabas' courageous challenge of Paul was not motivated by a desire to be right, to win the day or to one-up his leader. And his actions did not represent a power grab or an attempt for greater influence.

Barnabas was principle-driven; he was willing to risk confrontation with his leader and even a short-term loss of influence with Paul in order to defend the principles of leadership development, grace and forgiveness in ministry relationships. We have no record of Barnabas confronting Paul over other matters. Evidently, he was a loyal and faithful follower. But when essential principles were at stake, Barnabas was willing to stand his ground and challenge his leader.

Effective followers will ask themselves, *Does my obedience represent real submission to God and to God's appointed authority, or is it a desire to avoid conflict and serve my own interests? If I believed that essential principles were at stake, would I be willing to pursue gracious confrontation and submit to the consequences?* The next chapter will explore in greater detail how a follower can respond when he feels that a leader has stepped out of bounds on an essential principle.

To Let Them Lead

For those followers who have leadership gifts of their own, the greatest challenge in meeting a leader's needs may well be submitting over the long haul to the leader's direction and vision.

Followers who are marked by God for future leadership will be frustrated at times with the leadership of those they follow. The temptation to second-guess, criticize and even defy their leader will be a very real one, complicated at times by the fact that the follower may occasionally be right, or even more gifted as a leader than the leader he must follow!

These are the times when followers must keep close to God's heart and submit to His requirements for followership. We must keep close watch on the motivations of our hearts, monitor our speech and conduct and rely on the Holy Spirit for help moment by moment. Too many promising potential leaders have short-circuited or even destroyed their futures by impatience, ill-advised confrontation, manipulation and disrespect for those in authority. We should expect the temptations to come quickly and furiously, to be prone to rationalization and explanation and even to appear to be a brave, virtuous course of action. These lies must be exposed for what they are and rejected.

Humility is nothing more than unbridled realism. An effective follower is a realistic follower and hence a humble one. A leader serves by leading and a follower serves by following. For a follower to step outside the bounds which God has ordained is a disservice to the organization, the leader and, ultimately, God. As in all things, our model is Jesus, who, though He was God Himself, gave up divine privileges to become a servant (Philippians 2:5-7).

Followers who are comfortable with their role will meet their leaders' needs almost without trying.

There are two themes in this overview of some of the things leaders need from followers. First, the *heart motivation* of the follower precedes and shapes all conduct. Followers who are comfortable with their role, trusting God, seeking to live in obedience moment by moment and demonstrating confidence in their leaders will meet their leaders' needs almost without trying. Second, a follower must meet a leader's needs in a *transparent* way, so that his integrity is visible to the leader and to others within and without the organization.

One of the most painful challenges a follower can face is when he believes that the leader may have lost his right to lead through incompetence, poor judgment, lack of fidelity to biblical principles or moral compromise. We turn now to look at how we may conduct ourselves with integrity in what may be our most agonizing experience as a second fiddle.

Endnotes

1. Thomas McCann, *An American Company: The Tragedy of United Fruit* (New York: Crown, 1976), pp. 125-127.
2. John W. Gardner, *The Heart of the Matter* (Washington, DC: Independent Sector, 1986), p. 6.

Chapter
7

When a Leader May Be Wrong

Followers need to keep in balance all the qualities discussed in the previous chapter. But there are times when certain qualities are needed more than others; courage and truth-telling, for instance, are most important in those difficult times when a follower suspects that a leader is making a wrong decision.

Following when one is convinced the leader is wrong is one of the most difficult challenges for an effective follower, particularly when the course of action chosen by the leader may result in significant harm to the organization's mission.

As we have emphasized, effective followers are not passive or docile; it is an energetic activity, requiring hard work and even harder thought. And leaders are not automatically right, even if they have been called to a position of spiritual authority. Followers are responsible to hold the leader accountable to high standards of wisdom and judgment, as well as fidelity to the mission and vision of the organization.

Followers are responsible to hold the leader accountable to high standards of wisdom and judgment, as well as fidelity to the mission and vision of the organization.

But to oppose a leader is a perilous thing. Leaders have been called by God to their positions, at least presumably. Short of clear violations of scriptural standards of moral integrity, how is a follower to discern what constitutes effective following in a situation where it *seems* that the leader is choosing a wrong course? What separates active, courageous following from presumption and arrogance?

Professor of leadership Bobby Clinton offers this counsel:

> The most important relational insight I have learned is that subordinates must be very careful in their correction of those in authority over them. One needs to be more than just right on issues to correct such a leader. Rightness or

> wrongness is not the whole matter. Sometimes being right on certain issues is less important than maintaining a positive relationship.[1]

Clinton's advice is wise. On the other hand, our proper reluctance to challenge a leader's decisions or direction does not excuse us from the hard, active work of following and of holding the leader accountable. One study of followers found that when a leader asks a follower to do something they know is wrong, thirty percent of them will usually do it anyway.[2] This is unacceptable behavior for a Christ-follower. When we suspect a leader may be wrong, what should we do?

1. Overlook the problem if you can.

This suggestion seems counterintuitive. Why should we ignore the roots of a problem which may grow bigger over time? The counsel here is for caution and trust in the leader, his or her calling, and God. "A man's wisdom gives him patience," says the proverb (Proverbs 19:11). "It is to his glory to overlook an offense." This principle is true in leader-follower relationships as well. It is far better to overlook missteps and errors in judgment on the part of a leader unless they are repeated over time or they are so serious as to threaten the integrity of the leader or the organization.

Implied in this first step is a healthy mistrust of self. "He who hates correction is stupid," says another proverb (12:1), characteristically to the point. It is a good thing to acknowledge that our view of the situation may be different and less clear than that of the leader, and that our conclusions may be hasty or simply wrong. Waiting allows time for the situation to clarify and for the Holy Spirit to bring understanding and wisdom to our hearts.

2. Seek wise counsel.

Even when you become convinced that the leader is making a serious mistake, it is still not time to act. Next, it is important to subject your views to the loving criticism of a few well-chosen others. "Plans fail for lack of counsel, but with many advisers they succeed" (15:22).

If it is at all possible, choose a few individuals, well-removed from your situation, who have proven themselves trustworthy over time, and lay the situation out to them, seeking and acting upon their counsel. They should be people of integrity, prayer and proven wisdom—and *not* prone to gossip or fault-finding. And they must be willing and able to challenge you and to tell you hard truths about yourself.

If you have no one like this in your life, it is time to cultivate these kinds of relationships. Begin to pray that God will bring such people into your life; look for practical ways to expand your network of encouraging, supportive friendships.

3. Avoid a "take no prisoners" approach.

It is common among Christians, particularly in professional ministry and church circles, to pursue a policy of total annihilation in conflict. After all, we are talking about spiritual things, issues of eternal significance, right? Scripture and God's will are at stake here; those who disagree with us are failing to hear and obey God, we think.

And so we launch missiles when a gentle conversation would have been helpful. We end friendships and break fellowship when a simple one-hour meeting over coffee to clarify points of view might have averted conflict.

Don't give in to the notion that leader-follower conflicts are a winner-take-all game.

4. Go to the leader, presenting your case in terms he can understand.

You have done your homework patiently, given the leader the benefit of the doubt, sought the counsel of others, and you are still convinced that the leader is pursuing an unwise and damaging course.

It is time for you to confront the leader—gently, respectfully and in love. It is time to exercise what Robert Kelley calls the "courageous conscience," where you are able to judge right from wrong and, most importantly, act accordingly. To do this, you must hold in tension your convictions and the possibility that you may be wrong and that the leader may have a perfectly good reason why he has chosen his course of action.

It is important here to make a distinction between routine, or *formative,* confrontation and crisis-point, or *summative,* confrontation. Formative confrontation is part of a gentle, ongoing process where feedback is given and received in a gracious, constructive way. It is the primary responsibility of the leader to create an environment where formative confrontation can happen as an ongoing part of life together. And if you are a follower, it is your responsibility to take advantage of such a climate, giving and receiving criticism with a gracious, open spirit.

You must hold in tension your convictions and the possibility that the leader may have a perfectly good reason why he has chosen his course of action.

"John, I noticed that you cut Susan off in the meeting today," a formative confrontation might begin. "You know, I've seen you do this in the last couple weeks, which I know have been a stressful time for you. You might want to pay attention to that."

Summative confrontation comes at a crisis or semi-crisis point and is much more serious in nature. As the name implies, summative confrontation sums up a list of grievances or acts of wrongdoing which have taken place over time. Summative confrontation usually marks a change in the nature of the relationship and may indicate that the future of the relationship itself is in question.

"John, over the last year, you have repeatedly belittled and snapped at your employees. You have made them feel unimportant and intimidated. The fact that half of your department has resigned in the last two years indicates an ongoing problem. It is time for you to consider what this means; you need to respond to some specific concerns that I have. How you respond may well determine if you and I can continue to work together."

Ideally, summative confrontation should never take place. If John is a man of integrity and his followers are people of boldness and courage, his abusive behavior would have been noted and dealt with early on.

But summative confrontation is sometimes unavoidable. When this is the case, it is important, before you do the confronting, to examine your motives carefully, making sure that you are not pursuing this course of action out of a desire to undermine your leader for your own gain, to increase your power and influence or to reap revenge or self-justification.

5. Work for resolution and serve the leader.

The narrative of Acts 15 is proof that even seemingly hopeless situations can end in reconciliation and peace. The fledgling church nearly split apart over the question of whether non-Jews had to become Jews by circumcision before they could be true Christians. The battle was pitched and intense, raising emotional questions of culture, theology and relationships.

A church council was convened in Jerusalem to settle the question. What unfolded next (Acts 15:6-31) is a model of creative and spiritually attentive conflict resolution. The elders considered each case, heard and applied Scripture, gave prayerful thought to the outcome, arrived at resolution and took steps to insure that the reconciliation lasted. They were able to put their own ideas, convictions and agendas aside and listen to what the Spirit had to say to the church. This process, under God, did nothing less than save the church from an irreconcilable division.

These principles can be applied to interpersonal relationships as well as church councils. A careful, respectful, humble, prayerful and deliberate process of listening and negotiating can bring about resolution. Leaders can own up to their mistakes; followers can see things in a new way. Relational bonds can be preserved and even strengthened. I have seen this happen, as a follower and as a leader. It is sweet and faith-affirming.

From a distance, I have watched the opposite happen, when followers are contentious and contemptuous, when leaders are disrespectful and obstinate. The resulting pain and turmoil scars lives, ministries and churches, and damages the image of the body of Christ.

Perhaps the hardest thing to do during this time is to maintain the priority of serving your leader. You are convinced that he is wrong and is embarking on a dangerous course; you are beginning to doubt his credibility. It may be everything you can do not to run into his office and shout, "Stop the madness!" But frankly, you must, even at this difficult time, keep your heart focused on your calling to count his interests more important than your own and to serve him in love. This will give you a strong credibility—even in the midst of your resistance to what you believe to be wrong—that you could not have in any other way. And your heart will be pleasing to God, which is more important still.

A careful, respectful, humble, prayerful and deliberate process of listening and negotiating can bring about resolution.

6. Leave with integrity.

You hope and pray, of course, that you never have to come to this final step. But it's important to think through what you will do if it becomes clear that the leader continues on what you believe to be a wrong course, in spite of the counsel and prayer of others.

Sabotaging the leader or orchestrating a palace coup is not an option. These kinds of strategies, so common in the political and corporate worlds, have no place among followers of Christ, the gentle Servant without pretense or guile.

If it becomes clear that the situation will not change, you may choose to remove yourself from the situation. How can you do this in a kind and loving way, a way that preserves your integrity and has the best chance of retaining a healthy relationship with your leader?

First, tell the leader you are leaving before you tell anyone else. Have a face-to-face meeting, whether you are leaving a job, resigning from a committee or choosing to join another church. Voice or e-mail messages, memos and letters are not adequate forms of communication at a time like this, unless the leader has demonstrated such abusive or unpredictable behavior that you literally would fear for your safety. Leave quietly, resisting the temptation to depart with a dramatic, image-enhancing flourish. You will most likely simply look foolish!

Next, as you communicate with others, emphasize the positive aspects of both the leader and your own experience serving under the leader. Except for cases of compromised moral integrity, which we will discuss in the next chapter, you should never say anything publicly that in any way casts doubt on the character or competence of the leader—as tempting as it may be to explain your actions or to retaliate. This is kindness and caring for your neighbor, two things very near to God's heart. This is also wisdom, for we can be sure that we will be treated in the same way we choose to treat others.

Finally, there are things you should do even after you have left:

- Make it a priority to continue to pray for the leader.
- Take the opportunity to examine your own heart, asking God to show you where you may be mistaken or even wrong.
- Take the time to journal about your experience, noting things you want to remember for future situations in which you will be either a follower or leader.

It is never a pleasant experience to confront a leader who has erred. We are tempted to take the course of least resistance, covering over errors of judgment or failings in an attempt to keep a false peace and protect ourselves. If we succumb to this temptation, we are failing our organization and our leader. But we may also be tempted toward the opposite error—rushing to quick conclusions and confrontations. Giving in to either temptation is a dangerous compromise of our integrity and can create both personal and organizational disunity.

But if we act with courage and compassion, exercising the "courageous conscience" we have disciplined ourselves to develop, our differences with our leaders can lead to creative resolution at the most, or honest, clean disagreement at the least.

Endnotes

1. J. Robert Clinton, *The Making of a Leader* (Colorado Springs, CO: NavPress, 1988), p. 106.
2. Robert Kelley, *The Power of Followership* (New York: Doubleday, 1992), p. 171.

Chapter

8

When a Leader Fails

All-staff meetings were rare, particularly in the middle of the week. But the message had gone out over the church's voice-mail system, requesting that all program staff convene in the conference room immediately for an important meeting.

As the group gathered, Dick realized that, like him, none of his colleagues knew the reason for the meeting. There was a slightly anxious buzz in the room, punctuated occasionally by nervous, too-loud laughter. Dick was a bit annoyed by the fact that, as the senior associate, he hadn't been informed about the meeting ahead of time.

The door opened and Jim, the church's pastor, and Ted, the head elder, walked into the room. Both had strained expressions on their faces. Dick noticed that

Jim appeared to have aged a decade since he had last seen him, two weeks ago.

"Folks, we have a very difficult and painful announcement to make today," Bill began. "The elder board this morning received Pastor Jim's resignation, which is effective immediately." Ted paused for a moment to let the shock wash over the assembled staff.

"Pastor Jim has resigned because of a series of moral failings and missteps he has made over the past two years. He has repented of these sins and has submitted to a restoration process, but it has become clear to all of us that he has compromised his integrity to the point where he is no longer able to lead this congregation. We are going to provide counseling and financial assistance for Jim and Sally, but he is stepping aside today as our pastor. Jim, I think, has a few words to say to you all."

The pastor, normally a graceful man, stepped haltingly to the end of the conference table. He cleared his throat several times, adjusted his tie, took off and replaced his glasses and finally began to speak in a thin, fragile voice.

"I have failed and betrayed you. I have let this congregation down. Most of all, I have let the Lord down. I know that His forgiveness is available to me and I have asked for that, but I also know that my actions have taken a terrible toll on my family and, beginning today, they will on this church as well. And on many of you."

He continued. "I blame no one but myself for what I have done. I sinned—I made the choice to disregard what God said in some key areas of my life. If I could relive the last two years, I would. And the first thing I would do is make sure that there were those in my life with the right to call me up short, to challenge me, to hold me accountable. I have failed in many ways, but one of the greatest is that I have not called others around me who would speak the truth in love."

Dick felt as if the floor were dropping out from under him. In a moment, the truth hit him with icy, devastating force. He had suspected for a number of months what was going on. On more than one occasion, he had had reason to believe that Jim was engaging in inappropriate behavior. More than once, he had opened his mouth to question Jim, only to swallow his words. The stakes were too high, the damage to his position and influence too great if he was wrong. Besides, he had never liked conflict much.

Sin Happens

Leaders fail, often and with sometimes devastating consequences. The late 1980s and early 1990s brought this realization home to American evangelicals with particular force as a succession of high profile leaders lost their ministries and credibility over sexual misconduct and financial improprieties.

We feign shock at times, but a moment's consideration should cause us to get over that. "The heart is deceitful above all things and beyond cure," said the prophet Jeremiah a long time ago. "Who can understand it?" (Jeremiah 17:9).

Sin happens or, more accurately, people sin, especially those who think they can't or won't. Leaders are particularly susceptible to "big-ticket" sins, for several reasons.

For one, Satan can get a lot of mileage from the fall of a Christian leader, particularly if his fall is connected to a "juicy" sin like greed or lust.

For another, leaders are often people whose egos are constantly being stroked. Unless God grants a strong dose of humility, fueled by diligent use of the spiritual disciplines of repentance, confession and self-examination, leaders can begin to believe their own press.

And the nature of leadership is to be alone at times. It is when we are alone and perhaps lonely that the voice of the tempter—promising power and relief, and preying on our sense of entitlement and self-pity—can be so alluring.

Followers are hurt when a leader stumbles: Dreams die, illusions are shattered, futures are cast into doubt.

With Painful Consequences

When leaders fall, they leave a trail of wreckage in their wake. Followers are hurt when a leader stumbles: Dreams die, illusions are shattered, futures are cast into doubt. The stakes are high, with potential for long-term damage.

For followers put into this most painful situation, there is also a unique opportunity to see more clearly the sustaining grace of God. When our leader has fallen or is in danger of falling, we can choose to deny what is happening, to cover-up the leader's misdeeds or to act in self-protective ways. Or we can be tender, vulnerable, courageous and wise, facing up to the reality of our leader's brokenness and our own, and living out God's relentless, stubborn, forgiving grace.

Before the Fall

King David was on a roll, at the height of his powers, buoyed by political and military success and public acclaim. "David is at his prime," writes Eugene Peterson, "his body hard and sinewy, his mind sharply alert, his spirit blazing in worship and obedience."[1]

David was in love with God, His people and His kingdom, and he wanted to erect a fitting monument to his loves—a great temple, a fitting house for a great God. He called his advisor/prophet/pastor Nathan—his *follower* Nathan—and told him of his plans.

At first blush, Nathan was excited. It was a great idea, after all, to build a great house for God. Why not? "Go for it, king," he said.

Then Nathan went home and slept on it, praying over it. God checked his response and gave him a direct message to take back to the king.

God's message was along these lines: *Look, David, do I need a house? And do I need you to build it for Me? I have not asked for this; you have dreamed it up. Now, I will have a beautiful house one day—a temple to end all temples—but you are not the one to build it. Your ambition, My son, comes not from Me but from you. If you build this house you will be laying the foundation for your own ruin. I am the Housebuilder, not you. Don't ever forget that. Learn it well.* (See 2 Samuel 7:4-16.)

Nathan gulped and took the message back to David. To his credit, the king halted his grand scheme and placed himself humbly before the Lord in prayer; he stepped back from the cliff and avoided the fall. He had been saved by words of truth from the mouth of a courageous follower.

Nathan's actions demonstrate how a follower can help a leader who is in danger of a fall of any kind, whether connected to competence, moral integrity or relational strain.

He speaks the truth boldly in love, holding in check his own desire to be in the good graces of the leader and speaking only after he has filtered his words through God's Word and prayer.

Nathan was willing to speak boldly and confidently—and he had to. David, a man of action, was on a fast-moving train. Nathan had to meet the king's determination with determination of his own.

We should notice at least two things here:

1. Nathan's outspokenness carried a great amount of personal risk. In those days, you did not disagree with a monarch, particularly if you wanted to keep your head! Arguing with a king in the ancient Near East usually meant you had a death wish.

2. Nathan was willing to admit that *he* had been wrong as well. His first response to David's plan was enthusiastic: "Whatever you have in mind, go ahead and do it, for the LORD is with you" (2 Samuel 7:3). Later, when he heard otherwise from God, he was willing to admit a personal shortcoming in confronting the king.

Nathan's confrontation was a balance of boldness and humility. He knew how high the stakes were—the king's heart and the future of the kingdom—and he spoke clearly and directly. Followers who suspect that their leaders are on the road to a fall have to speak with this same boldness, for the stakes are high in those situations, too.

> Followers who suspect that their leaders are on the road to a fall have to speak with boldness, for the stakes are high.

The ministries and lives of leaders and those they lead, the reputation of Christ and of Christians in the community—all of these are damaged, often significantly, by leaders who abuse trust, slip morally, or squander resources. When your leader is close to the brink of failure, it is the wrong time to be considering one's own comfort and prestige.

Boldness, however, does not imply arrogance or a judgmental spirit. When we suspect that a leader is nearing a fall, our first response must be to critique our own perceptions carefully. Are we missing something? Giving a wrong interpretation to raw data? Choosing to believe the worst rather than the best?

When we become convinced that our fears and concerns are founded, however, we have to take action to confront our leader.

This confrontation must be *gentle,* creating an environment where the leader can admit fault without being condemned or shamed.

It must be *hopeful,* pointing the way for God to redeem the situation or at least the hearts of those involved.

It must be *realistic,* neither glossing over wrongdoing or giving an apocalyptic cast to a simple mistake.

And finally, the confrontation must be *humble,* as you realize that, given a similar set of circumstances and pressures, you could make the same mistakes.

If your leader is going to fall, may it never be because his trusted followers were afraid to tell him the hard truth—or worse yet, because they told him the truth, but in a way that he couldn't understand or accept.

After the Fall

At the height of his power, King David fell like few others in history have fallen. Restless, bored, neglecting his duty to lead his troops into battle, David manipulated and forced a young woman, Bathsheba, to have an affair with him. When she became pregnant, he brought her soldier husband back from the battlefield, hoping that he and his wife would sleep together and cover up the king's adultery. But David didn't bargain for the husband, Uriah, to be a man of conscience and duty, one who would refuse to sleep with his wife in the comfort of their home while his compatriots were still on the front lines.

His plan foiled, the desperate king resorted to murder. He had Uriah placed directly in the line of fire during the battle and, predictably, the soldier was killed.

After a suitable time of mourning, David married the widow Bathsheba, doubtless breathing a sigh of relief that he had covered up a potentially explosive situation with no one the wiser. He had lusted, committed adultery, lied, manipulated and murdered, this "man after God's own heart." But no one knew.

Except God. And Nathan.

God is often crafty and cunning, though only in the purest of ways. God sent Nathan to spin an outrageous story of a rich man who owned many sheep but who stole the only sheep a poor man possessed. Properly indignant, the king demanded justice for one who had stolen without conscience and pity.

Then Nathan spoke four of the most pointed, devastating words in the Bible: "You are the man!" Nathan's story was designed to expose the king's heart and his sin, to break past his defenses and bring conviction of sin.

Nathan's words hit their mark. The king was broken; he repented and handled with consummate grace the horrible consequences of his sin, including the death of

Bathsheba's child and the horrible dysfunctions in much of the rest of his family (2 Samuel 11-12).

The king took a hard fall, brought about by his own actions, but for the remainder of his life he was a different man. Less impressive in his appearance, less sinewy, alert and strong, the king was a wiser, sadder, more gentle man. All of this, in part, because of the wounds inflicted on him by a faithful follower.

What did Nathan say and do that made the difference after the fall?

First, like God, he was *cunning*. Again, this is an odd word to apply to God, but no other word will do. God knows how we can erect barriers to understanding and change, filters which keep us from hearing the truths about ourselves we need so desperately to hear. And so the Holy Spirit works to penetrate our defenses, get a foot in the door, open a small crack so that truth can rush in and flood the darkened corners of our lives.

Dan Allender and Tremper Longman describe our condition, the stark condition of a falling or fallen person, as well as the severe remedy which God applies:

> Our hearts are poisoned . . . toward worshipping God, because our bent is toward serving other gods, and He will not share His glory. He is intolerant of a divided heart; therefore, He works mysteriously and often ruthlessly to destroy all that violates true worship and love.[2]

This is exactly what God was up to in David's life, and He used the follower Nathan, who wanted his leader's welfare so bad that he was willing to risk his own life to accomplish it. If your leader is guilty of sin, make yourself available to God to move with creativity and humility to press the truth home to him. Perhaps no one else can or will do this.

Again, he was *bold*. News accounts of President Bill Clinton's White House have noted that aides often jockeyed to avoid the duty of telling their boss bad news about the personal scandals that crippled his presidency. The worst fate that could befall a White House aide is likely loss of his job.

If your leader is guilty of sin, make yourself available to God to move with creativity and humility to press the truth home to him.

By pointing his finger at the king and crying out, "You are the man!" Nathan could have lost his head. But he was so committed to truth, integrity and, not incidentally, his leader, that he was willing to take that risk. We don't know too much about him, but we do know that Nathan was a follower possessed of unusual courage.

But as impressive as Nathan's courage is his *compassion*. Nathan speaks God's words, denouncing David in the strongest of terms. At the end, David has only one short sentence by way of reply: "I have sinned against the LORD." We can almost feel the ironic, iron tenderness in Nathan's reply: "The LORD has taken away your sin. You are not going to die." And then he goes ahead and announces the terrible consequences that will come: "The son born to you will die" (12:13-14).

There. That's it. Nathan the follower speaks words of tenderness and hard truth to his leader, acknowledging the gravity of the offense and the consequences of the offense, but offering the promise of God's forgiveness and restoration.

Overkill?

Perhaps you're thinking that this is all a bit much. In most situations, whether in the marketplace or the ministry, when a leader falls through moral compromise, financial wrongdoing or gross incompetence, he or she slinks away as the followers avert their eyes and try to pick up the pieces. Isn't all this talk of cunning and boldness, of compassion and courage, too much?

Yes, if we don't care about what God is up to in our lives, or the story He is telling in our midst. The human heart is the stage of God's great drama, and human relationships are the proving ground of what is going on inside. The way that we as followers respond to fallen leaders tells us everything about our own character and will have everything to do with how Jesus is perceived by those watching us.

Are we judgmental, cold and vengeful? Then that's what God looks like. Oblivious, denying and spineless? Then that's what God looks like. Bold, courageous, honorable, compassionate and cunning? Then that's what God looks like to the watching world.

These last two chapters have been difficult for me to write. As I finish them I do so with the prayer that none of us will ever fall ourselves or see our leader fall. But I sense that this is not a prayer the Lord will fully answer. Leaders will fall. How we respond to them and to God is critically important. Will we answer the challenge?

Endnotes

1. Eugene H. Peterson, *Leap Over a Wall* (New York: HarperCollins, 1997), p. 162.
2. Dan Allender and Tremper Longman, *Bold Love* (Colorado Springs, CO: NavPress, 1992), p. 209.

Chapter

9

Lessons from a Life of Followership

Principles in ink on a page are just that—ink on a page. To make a difference in our lives, principles have to be fleshed out in real life, that messy place where our aspirations and ideals collide with our failures and shortcomings.

For that reason, it is a good thing to point to examples of men and women who are living in accordance with the principles we aspire to follow in our own lives—men and women who set the pace, live with integrity and finish well. For our purposes, it would be a good thing to take a look into the life of a follower who follows with excellence.

Irv Chambers is such a follower. For more than forty years, Irv has been a faithful follower of Jesus Christ and a coworker with Leighton Ford, an internationally renowned Christian evangelist, author and leader. For years, Irv served alongside Leighton and others with the Billy Graham Evangelistic Association, helping to coordinate crusade rallies and often serving as worship leader and platform director. In more recent years, he served as a key administrator for Leighton Ford Ministries' evangelism and leadership development programs.

I spent an afternoon with Irv asking what it takes to follow so well for so long and what advice he has for younger followers. What strikes you about Irv, and other great followers, is how little they seem to realize their importance to the leader. You will see this servant-humility as you read Irv's reflections on a lifetime of ministry.

Q: You have devoted almost your entire career to serving and following one senior leader, Leighton Ford. When you look on your life as a follower and a leader in your own right, what stands out to you?

A: I've said to Marilyn [Irv's wife] a number of times in recent years how grateful I am for the opportunities of ministry that we have had—the privilege of working with Leighton, the Billy Graham Association, Leighton Ford Ministries, all of these things—which have taken us so many places and given us so many unique evangelistic opportunities. I feel very blessed to have worked with Leighton for forty-three years. It's been a great experience, and that's probably why it doesn't seem like almost half a century!

Q: You first met Leighton in 1956 and worked on a crusade together after you were introduced on the phone by a mutual friend. Did you know right away when you and he met that this was a man you could follow?

A: I think I came to that conclusion after being with him for a while. He is so articulate and practical in his presentation of the gospel. It was all very logical and each step led you to the next. I had worked with a number of evangelists before meeting Leighton and they weren't all as straightforward or reasonable in their speaking. Some relied on histrionics or death-bed stories to assure a full altar at the invitation. Leighton not only had a passion for evangelism, which I shared, but he also had an honorable and good presentation of the gospel. I never felt embarrassed or awkward after he spoke. And I thought, *Now here's a guy with whom I can really relate.* I was happy to be associated with him and with that kind of presentation of the gospel. He invited me to work with him some more and we found that there were a number of areas where we had complementary gifts. It just seemed like the Lord had brought us together and that this was the thing to do.

Q: You and Leighton have worked together intimately for many years. How has your relationship with him developed during that time?

A: Well, right from the start, I think we just hit it off well. We were not only compatible in theology, but in many ways—including a mutual desire to see people come to Christ. It was a mutual appreciation of gifts and certainly, for me, his presentation of the gospel; he is very gifted in this area and I was very comfortable with that. I've seen him at Kiwanis, Rotary and other secular civic clubs and never felt like he overstepped his bounds. I had been with some other speakers who went into similar situations and gave them "hell and brimstone" and there were some occasions where I said to myself, *They'll never invite another evangelist or preacher to that service club!*

But that wasn't true with Leighton. I always had the feeling he went to the point where he could go and made the clear presentation of the gospel, but not to the point of irritating or aggravating relationships with those people and killing any future opportunities of having a minister speak to the group. Our relationship went beyond ministry. Our families often spent holidays together, and some vacations. Leighton even "married" us—but we didn't take him on the honeymoon. You have to draw the line someplace!

Q: You have a great deal of professional respect for him.

A: Very much so, yes.

Q: Leighton is known as a remarkable leader. You have said that part of what makes him such an effective leader is his ability to adapt to his audience and to the different situations in which he finds himself. So, what are the gifts you as a follower bring to the relationship?

A: My gifts are more in the area of administration and organization, working with committees and board members. My original role in the crusades was as the music director, emceeing the crusade programs, planning the musical program, conducting the choir and recruiting guest musicians. As time went by I also got involved in organizing other aspects of the crusades—such things as stadium or auditorium rentals, recruiting choir members and prayer partners, working with finance and other committees. The objective was to plan for every possible

> How wonderful it is to work with someone whom you feel is a servant of the Lord and so gifted with the way he shares the good news!

eventuality so that things ran as smoothly as possible when the public meetings began.

Q: When you look back over your years of working with Leighton, if you had to isolate a few ways in which you were able as his follower to serve him most, what would they be?

A: Well, I think after you are with any person for a while, you begin to understand how they function, what they need to keep them from being distracted from their primary responsibility of presenting the gospel. It is a challenge to try and remove every obstacle or barrier that could serve as an interruption to the speaker or any part of the presentation. You obviously can't foresee everything, but you work as though you can. My goal was to do as much as I could to simplify things for Leighton. Obviously there were some failures, but with each failure there was learning and the promise that "I won't let that happen again."

How wonderful it is to work with someone whom you feel is a servant of the Lord and so gifted with the way he shares the good news! Leighton has feet of clay. . . . He is human. Now me? I've got feet *and legs* of clay! Perhaps one reason it has worked so well is because of his patience with me. No one is perfect, so accept the person you work with and see how together you can joyfully lift up and exalt our Lord.

Q: I want to ask you about Leighton's legacy, and then your own. First, Leighton's. What is the legacy he will leave after a lifetime of ministry?

A: I think Leighton is a leader of leaders and a preacher of preachers. He's got a good mind, he knows and has worked with many leaders. He has been called upon many times to recommend people for various positions: the president of a seminary, the pastor of a church or the leader of a para-church ministry. The unique thing about Leighton is that he doesn't just know people in his own age or peer group. He knows a lot of younger leaders who possess leadership skills. He has mentored many and I don't think there is anything that gives him more fulfillment than helping some young pastor or evangelist think and work through ministry opportunities.

At this point, I think his greatest legacy will be the development of young leaders. That's not to say that all that he did in the evangelistic crusades and with the Lausanne Committee was not important, but it prepared him so that he could have this ministry of mentoring and developing younger men and women who will be tomorrow's leaders in ministry.

Q: How do you share in that legacy? What have you done to help make that happen?

A: You know, I don't feel like I have done that much, other than support him and, hopefully, lighten his load in some areas so that he could more effectively use the other skills God has given him. It has been a great privilege and a unique opportunity to see God at work in very special ways.

Q: Is that legacy one that you're proud to be a part of?

A: Yes, I think that's all part of it. It is very encouraging to me because I think that a person is especially fulfilled when he or she is using and developing the gifts God has given. That brings great joy and satisfaction. And when you also see people come to Christ, you feel as though you have an investment in it. What could be more fulfilling?

A person is especially fulfilled when he or she is using and developing the gifts God has given.

Q: When has it been the hardest to follow Leighton?

A: One situation that comes to mind is when we were in another country on a secular university campus for a lunch-hour assembly where the mood seemed to be "get this evangelist and make him sorry he ever came to this campus." That day our team was the target of large fresh eggs and the most inventive four-letter words I had ever heard. It was toughest for Leighton. That was one day it was hard to follow Leighton, because of these difficulties, but one of those that I remember most fondly. But I was never prouder of Leighton as he made a simple and loving presentation that made an impact on that campus.

Obviously, with anyone you're going to have some disagreements. I've never had a disagreement with Leighton on anything I'd call major such as in theology. Sometimes, maybe on philosophy of ministry, but with him, I really felt like God had called him and I could support him and help him. I've had some differences sure, but maybe I would have taken his approach had I been the leader. I accepted the fact that he was the leader and the buck stopped there. As a follower or a leader it is important to put yourself in the other person's "shoes," to try and see it from his perspective.

Q: Can you think of a time when you had to do that?

A: Many years ago there was a time where he was questioning his gifts in ministry. We were in the midst of a difficult crusade. He felt empty as he stood to preach, and began to wonder about his call to ministry. In a case like that, you have a twofold anxiety. The first is, what's happening to my brother? And secondly, what's going to happen to my wife and family? You know, am I going to be out of a job? You are going to face difficulties in even the best of situations.

Q: How did you help Leighton during that time?

A: I don't feel that I was that big of a help with advice or words of affirmation. The most helpful thing I could do was just to be there for him. Jeanie [Leighton's wife] was there, which was fortunate because she is a great encourager. Sometimes availability can be the biggest help and the most important thing you can be or do.

Q: You are a veteran follower. Many of the readers of this book will just be beginning a lifetime of following. What advice do you have for them?

A: Find a leader that you respect, who is or will be a role model for you. He should be one whom you can learn from, and who is willing to teach you and make you his disciple or mentoree. Find somebody who will push and challenge you. I think of a friend of mine who, during his seminary years, spent his summers working on a church staff where they had a very wise pastor. Each summer the pastor gave him a different position and new responsibilities. One summer he worked with the youth, another in Christian education and another in another position. He was training that young man for the pastorate and gave him much practical experience. That seminary student today is one of our leading evangelical pastors.

Find a leader that you respect, who is or will be a role model for you.

Find somebody who can give you tools, different kinds of opportunities and who will challenge you with responsibility. In high school, I had a pastor who was probably more gifted as an evangelist than as a pastor. He preached, he played instruments, he sang. . . . He could do it all. And he was passionate about preaching the gospel anywhere and everywhere. In those days I was a trumpet player (allegedly!) and he used to take me along to some of these evangelistic meetings. I thought, *Hey, this is neat for me; it's a great opportunity*. I didn't realize it, but he was really discipling me all that time. And part of my passion for evangelism came from him, from those weekends during my high school years when I was out playing the horn and watching and listening to him. It's amazing what that did for me. Your life can also be a significant influence on others.

I would also say, go to your leader and tell him or her what you would like to get out of this job opportunity. Is this person willing to invest in your growth at the same time as you invest in this ministry? We all realize that a team effort can produce greater results than that of one person, provided they are going in the same direction.

Q: Now, imagine that you're speaking to leaders. What counsel do you have for them as they lead their followers?

A: First, find somebody who is not looking to take your job, but sees his gift as supportive and complementary. If he's looking for your job, and in a year sees that isn't going to happen, he will be gone! Be willing to invest in the training of people so that they can be more effective in the combined ministry you are called to. Encourage them to succeed, and celebrate their successes with them.

Second, give the follower enough information so that he can fulfill your mission; let him know what your limitations are. In other words, if you tell a follower to do a job, let that person know exactly what the job parameters are and what you want him or her to do. Is he to survey the situation and come back with three recommendations? Or is he to survey it, determine the best possible solution, work out a budget, submit it for approval and, once it is approved, proceed with the project until it is completed? Be specific—and be realistic! Help him to evaluate failures and to know the reason a project failed. How would you do this now that you have had this experience? Look for someone who shares and wants to buy into your vision.

Be an encouragement, not only to the follower, but to his family.

Help him to grow—challenge him!

Q: How old are you?

A: I turned seventy recently. Now, I *feel* more like forty-nine.

Q: Do you?

A: I always felt twenty-nine or thirty. I don't feel like I'm seventy. . . . I remember my seventh-grade teacher told the class he was twenty-seven years of age, and I thought that poor guy's got one foot in the grave. After being in ministry all these years, though, it doesn't seem that way now!

Chapter

10

A Word to Leaders

The leading players in the New Testament—after Jesus, of course—are the apostles and the other early leaders of the church. They wrote the books of the New Testament; they provided the key leadership that helped the gospel take root and spread in its early days.

But every movement, no matter how dynamic, is exactly one generation away from extinction. The writing, preaching and leading of the apostles was no more important than their investment in the lives of others who would follow them.

Consider these hard facts:

- Two out of five followers feel that their leaders have questionable qualifications to lead.

- Less than half of all leaders are able to instill trust in their followers.
- Only one in seven leaders is someone that followers see as a role model.[1]

Leaders can make or break a movement, church, business or ministry by how they treat, invest in and prepare their followers for future leadership. This chapter breaks from the rest of the book in that it directly addresses leaders, not followers. My assumption is that some readers of this book function more in a leadership role than a followership role and are reading this book because they want to understand those who follow them.

If this describes you, thanks for reading! My guess is that you are asking questions such as these:

- What does it take to lead in such a way that others will want to follow?
- What do my followers need from me?
- How can I insure that the values with which I lead continue if I am called somewhere else?

We're going to take a few moments to explore these questions.

Timothy—Understudy to a Leading Player

It's tough to follow a great leader. The pressure to match up, meet expectations, maintain standards of excellence and serve a high-octane leader can be intense.

Imagine being Timothy, called to follow Paul—a volatile, passionate, gifted, world-class leader. Who just happened to be called to be the most significant leader of the early church.

We don't know much about Timothy. What little information we have comes from the two New Testament letters Paul wrote to him—and much of our knowledge comes from reading between the lines. We know that Timothy had been blessed with a godly family heritage, that he was timid by nature and that he struggled with some health problems.

> Paul's letters serve as a model for leaders who want to serve their followers well.

We see Timothy's character most clearly in the personal encouragement Paul gives him. Paul's words focus on clinging tightly to faith in Christ, holding to his call, standing firm in the face of opposition. The impression we get is that Timothy had a pure heart, a sensitive spirit, and may have been prone to fear and discouragement. Hardly a match for his tempestuous, bold, conflict-relishing mentor!

But Paul was the man God had made him to be, and Timothy was the one whom God had appointed to follow Paul most closely and to serve as Paul's heir apparent, particularly in his role as leader of the Ephesian church.

Paul's letters to Timothy reveal the heart of a leader who loves his follower, who knows that the stakes involved in mentoring are high and who shepherds a protégé with integrity, care and skill. His letters serve as a model for leaders who want to serve their followers well. And they offer a glimpse into the mentoring "toolbox" of a master leader.

This chapter presumes that you desire to be a mentor, not just a boss, and that you care more about your followers' lives than their productivity. If this is the case, here are a few tools you might want to consider adding to your own toolbox.

Know Your Followers' Hearts and Show Them Yours

Paul was a man of passion, and this came out in everything he said, did and wrote. As an effective leader, he also knew how to communicate his passion to his followers. "But you know what I teach, Timothy," he wrote, "and how I live and what my purpose in life is. You know my faith and how long I have suffered. You know my love and my patient endurance" (2 Timothy 3:10, NLT).

This passage comes in the middle of a section in which Paul is giving Timothy a stern challenge to stand courageously against false teachers. His admonition is not given from a safe spot on the hill above the battle.

Paul took false teaching very seriously and had the scars to prove it. The clarity of his message was of utmost importance to him and he was willing to pay any price to protect the gospel's integrity. He calls Timothy to join him in this fight, and he gives evidence from his own life that he practices what he preaches.

Think for a moment how Timothy would have heard Paul's message if it hadn't come with personal investment. Suppose Paul gave his orders in a dry, impersonal form: "Timothy, a big part of your job is to challenge these false teachers. That's what you're called to do, and I expect you to carry out your task. Get to it!" There's no life in this kind of direction, no passion.

Followers may obey a leader who commands without heart but only out of duty, fear or self-interest. Passionless leaders who do not reveal their own hearts will never capture the hearts and minds of their followers for a greater purpose.

Or suppose Paul had given his orders in passionate terms, but without personal investment: "Go wage war for the gospel, Timothy! The life and faith of the church hangs on what you do. When I get back from my vacation and from entertaining key supporters of the ministry, I want to hear all about it."

Again, a follower may respond in the short run to impersonal orders, but this won't last. *If my leader isn't willing to invest and risk personally,* reasons a follower, *why should I?* And the follower is right.

A leader's toolbox must include the skill of communicating vision and direction with passion, along with the integrity to live in such a way that followers know that the leader is in the game right beside them, facing the same challenges, working the same hours and paying the same (or greater) price.

The very best leaders move from communicating their own vision and passion to learning to know and care for their followers' hearts as well. It would be easy for us to assume that Paul wasn't a "people person," that he was a hard-charging, vision-driven, task-oriented leader who was largely unconcerned with the personal lives of his followers. It's fair to say that many leaders who seem to get the most done have this personality profile.

One of the elements which distinguishes a great leader from a very good one is the practice of knowing and caring for his or her followers in extravagant, surprising and affirming ways.

But not the highest level of leaders. One of the elements which distinguishes a great leader from a very good one is the practice of knowing and caring for his or her followers in extravagant, surprising and affirming ways.

After addressing Timothy as "my dear son," Paul goes on to write: "Timothy, I thank God for you. . . . Night and day I constantly remember you in my prayers. I long to see you again, for I remember your tears as we parted. And I will be filled with joy when we are together again" (2 Timothy 1:3-4, NLT).

Think for a moment about what it would be like to hear words like these, sincerely spoken, by someone you respected, followed and wanted to please. When someone expresses that they care for, enjoy and value us for who we are, not for what we can do, something powerful and good within us is released. Our loyalty and desire to serve that person grows naturally; a personal bond is formed and cemented which can survive later failures and misunderstanding.

Words like these are means of grace and they are so powerful because they reflect the grace of God given us in Jesus. Jesus' message to us, by His words and life, is how much He loves us and the great lengths to which He is willing to go to demonstrate that love.

When this extravagant grace meets a hungry, broken heart there is a response of awe, surprise, temporary disbelief and loving response. At our moments of greatest clarity, when we realize just what it means that Jesus lived and died for us, we know that there is nothing we would not do for Him if He asked us.

Christian leaders are called first to receive this grace in their own lives, and then to give it away to others. Grace-giving leaders who care deeply about the dreams, hopes and fears of their followers create reservoirs of loyalty, love, dedication and sacrifice that not only extend the mission and cause of the leader but meet some of the followers' deepest needs for significance, security and fulfillment.

Wise leaders will know their followers' hearts, care about their lives and be interested in the details of their day-to-day world. It is no accident that, just after writing his passionate greeting in his second letter to Timothy, Paul went on to make reference to Timothy's family (1:5). Paul was a leader who not only revealed his own heart to his followers, but took the time to know and cultivate theirs. So should leaders today.

Give Your Followers Clear Direction

Followers are happiest when they know what is expected of them, know that they have the resources they need and know that they have the support of their leader.

Paul excelled at giving clear direction to Timothy and providing him with the resources he needed to carry out his assignments. Paul's letters are models of lean, terse, clear directives:

> Teach these things and insist that everyone learn them. Don't let anyone think less of you because you are young. . . . Until I get there, focus on reading the Scriptures to the church, encouraging the believers, and teaching them. . . . But you, Timothy, belong to God; so run from all these evil things, and follow what is right and

> good. . . . And I command you before God . . . that you obey his commands with all purity. (1 Timothy 4:11-13; 6:11, 13-14, NLT)

There is no mistaking what Timothy is supposed to do or the resources he has to help him do it.

Paul was a focused leader, consumed with extending the kingdom of God through planting churches, developing leaders and defending the faith against false teachers. He expected his followers to hold these same values and to go about bringing them into reality. When a follower of Paul woke up in the morning, he knew what his priorities were for the day.

If you are a leader, make sure that your toolbox contains the skills of clear communication and unwavering support.

It is important to note that, while a leader will be clear and directive, he will also be willing to receive and, when appropriate, act on input from his followers. John Gardner notes, "Wise leaders are continuously finding ways to say to their constituents, 'I hear you.' "[2]

Such clear, focused and sensitive direction results in security, confidence and a feeling of accomplishment. If you are a leader, make sure that your toolbox contains the skills of clear communication—making your expectations known and listening to your followers' feedback—and unwavering support, both personal and corporate.

Give Your Followers Opportunity to Grow and Lead

Effective leaders always give their followers a little more to do than they think they can handle, and always push them a little farther than they feel ready to go. Always.

There is a fine line between challenging followers and exploiting them, but effective leaders know how to walk it. There is an art to knowing just how much a follower can stretch to accomplish new things and at what point that follower will be overwhelmed. Going too far can drive followers into failure and discouragement, and effective leaders know when to push and when to relent.

How far is too far? While there is no clear-cut answer, I encourage you to observe three working principles:

- Make sure your follower has all the necessary resources—time, contacts, staff, money—to accomplish any assigned task.
- Make sure that the task is within the sphere of the follower's calling and gifts.
- Make sure that accomplishing the task goes beyond mere productivity and results in the follower's personal growth and development.

Paul's letters to Timothy illustrate how a master leader calls a follower to greatness and pushes him beyond his area of comfort and experience with a firm yet gentle hand. The key to being able to do this is not only the personal investment we have already discussed but also the careful deployment of resources to help the follower know and accomplish the mission. We'll take a glance at some of those resources.

Mastering the Discipline

In a world where work and ministry require increasingly specialized skills, the importance of long-term, well-supervised apprenticeships are crucial. A good leader identifies what a follower needs to know to do the job. More importantly, a good leader discerns what the follower *doesn't* know but *needs* to know. This gap between experienced knowledge and necessary knowledge is filled when the leader, presumably more experienced than the follower, helps the follower master the discipline at hand.

Mastering the discipline involves knowing the ground rules, pitfalls, important players and keys to success in a given field. These lessons can only come with experience, and effective leaders make available their own experience—including their failures—to their followers.

Paul reminded Timothy of the "pattern of sound teaching" he had given him for his ministry (2 Timothy 1:13-14). This was a specific body of knowledge, passed from leader to follower, which was necessary for the follower's growth and success. Every discipline has such a body of knowledge and insight; selfless leaders willingly pass this on, saving their followers time and heartache.

Setting Priorities

These days, no one has enough time to do the things they need to do, much less want to do—at least, that's the way it seems. The fact is, we do have adequate time to do the things God has called us to do, but our complex lives present an often bewildering array of options, leaving us pulled, stressed and harried. A prerequisite to effective followership and leadership is knowing how to manage time and establish priorities.

A prerequisite to effective followership and leadership is knowing how to manage time and establish priorities.

Imagine an airline pilot saying something like this to the passengers over the intercom: "Folks, in just a few moments we'll be leaving New York and reach a cruising altitude of 30,000 feet. After that, though, we're not really sure what's next. We could go to Chicago; the weather is nice there. Or maybe Dallas, so my co-pilot can visit his parents. Or we might want to go to Big Sur, because the surf's up! We're not sure where our final destination will be, but we're going to look at all the alternatives and reach a decision sometime before we run out of fuel."

That's not going to happen, because it's the pilot's job to know where he's going and how to get there. A pilot has an enormous responsibility, which includes the safety of an airplane full of people, and he or she will be quick to eliminate any distractions that interfere with the mission: getting the plane safely to its appointed destination, hopefully on time.

The people who work for me tell me that one way I can help them the most is by giving them clear priorities. My assistant, Jennifer Hibbert, is particularly insistent on this point. "Tell me what we most need to focus on," she says, "and we'll get there. But we can't get there if you don't tell me." (Sometimes it's not entirely clear who is best qualified to lead in my office!)

Paul gave Timothy crystal clear priorities: "Do not waste time arguing over godless ideas and old wives' tales. Spend your time and energy in training yourself for spiritual fitness" (1 Timothy 4:7, NLT). This is a model statement for leaders, because it tells a follower what to focus on and, just as importantly, what not to waste time and energy on.

Facing Up to Obstacles

It's a cliché, but nonetheless true for the repetition: *Nothing worth doing is done easily.* This is especially so in spiritual leadership and followership; obstacles are inevitable in the form of spiritual attack, resistance to change, limited resources and garden-variety sin. Effective leaders know the obstacles facing their followers and give them plenty of warning. They also offer whatever help they can.

Paul was straight with Timothy: The obstacles he would face included suffering, persecution, false teaching and even spiritual inertia—in other words, some folks just don't respond to truth if it means changing their lives (2 Timothy 2:3; 4:3). Paul gave Timothy ample warning about the obstacles in his path and offered him three resources: a recollection of Timothy's own spiritual calling and gifting (1 Timothy 4:14); the all-sufficient teaching of Scripture (2 Timothy 3:16-17); and Paul's own assistance and instruction (1 Timothy 3:14-15).

It goes without saying that in order to know what obstacles a follower will face, a leader must be experienced and engaged in the work the follower is assigned to do. No one can lead in theory.

Defining Reality

Business leader and author Max DePree is well known for this helpful description of the bookend tasks of a leader: The first job of a leader is to define reality, and the last is to say thank you.[3]

The ability to define reality for one's followers is a high-level leadership skill. The fact is that things are not as they appear to most of us most of the time. A leader, particularly a spiritual leader, is one who sees things that others don't, sees more than others do, sees more clearly than others see and then is able to help others catch the same vision.

A creative leader opens up possibilities for his followers that they would never have guessed existed and invites them to enter the doorway to a new experience. I can't emphasize enough that this is to be normal leadership behavior, not something limited to the most exceptional leaders.

Do not take your unique position for granted if you lead others.

Paul defined reality for Timothy when he wrote, "For God did not give us a spirit of timidity, but a spirit of power, of love and of self-discipline" (2 Timothy 1:7). Timothy was a timid man, facing strong opposition and great challenges. But Paul didn't pay much attention to this. He was quick to define the reality beyond the reality: God was wholly able, even though Timothy was unable; God's strength would be seen most clearly as it overcame Timothy's weakness. The reality behind the reality was a powerful God who always accomplishes His purpose; that was Paul's point of emphasis.

Allowing Your Followers to Serve You

Many leaders have a hard time being led. Many servants have a hard time being served. But maturity demands that leaders follow and servants are served. The vulnerability of leadership sounds almost paradoxical. Instead, it is a secret of great strength. The later writer Henri Nouwen's well-known description of the "wounded healer" is a wonderful description of authentic spiritual leadership in this age which is so in tune with the brokenness of humankind.

There is a poignant difference between First Timothy and Second Timothy. In the first letter, Paul is brimming with confidence as he challenges Timothy to counter false teachers. In the second, he is in prison (probably under Emperor Nero) and it is clear that he is nearing the end of his life. It is possible that Second Timothy was the last letter Paul ever wrote.

Paul is still confident in Christ, but he is aware of his own mortality and how quickly his own time of influence and leadership is coming to an end. He tries to pack everything into this letter, leaving every bit of wisdom and encouragement he can.

The contrast between the two letters is never more clear than when Paul speaks of their distance. In First Timothy, Paul is determined to get to Timothy as soon as he can and has only written the letter as a stopgap measure in case he is delayed (3:14-15). In Second Timothy, he nearly begs Timothy to "do your best to come to me quickly," and then goes on to detail his loneliness (4:9 ff.). In the first letter, he is the confident leader on his way to save the day again, dashing off correspondence on the fly. In the last letter, he is older, graver, wiser, still full of hope but more in touch with his own need. He is, quite frankly, more attractive as a human being.

Paul the leader learned to admit his own vulnerability even while maintaining an unconquerable confidence in God's strength and power. One can only imagine how quick Timothy must have been to respond.

Recently, I was on a long airplane flight with several colleagues and a ministry team. We were returning from a time of great ministry, but I was tired, a little discouraged and, strangely, quite lonely. I know now that God was shifting things around in my soul to prepare me to love and serve Him better, but at the time I was just confused and a little scared.

I was seated next to one of my colleagues, a person whom I have been privileged to serve and invest in for several years. This colleague and friend has blossomed into ministry and is seen now as a strong spiritual leader; many follow this person.

Yet, I had never considered allowing this person to serve me. In fact, I would have gone to great lengths to do just the opposite. It was my job, I reasoned, to serve my colleagues and to help each of them develop as a person and a leader. My own needs were met in other places.

Yet on this long plane flight, God used this friend and colleague to speak comfort, challenge and truth to me. In a very real way, my friend was the means of grace God sent to tell me that He loved me and was not far from me.

I was a leader, but I was served well by a follower—a follower who has continued to follow and who later expressed joy at seeing, in that moment, a side of my humanness that was appealing. It was not a pretty side, I can tell you, but it was real. And God used that openness to build a follower's confidence and faith, and to humble and soften a leader.

Leaders, under God, may well be the most important factor in shaping the hearts of followers. Do not take your unique position for granted if you lead others. Do not fail to serve and love your followers with everything in you, with every resource God gives you. In doing this, you will find that your own heart is filled and your own calling is advanced.

Endnotes

1. Robert Kelley, *The Power of Followership* (New York: Doubleday, 1992), p. 201.
2. John W. Gardner, *The Heart of the Matter* (Washington, DC: Independent Sector, 1986), p. 5.
3. Max DePree, *Leadership Is an Art* (New York: Dell, 1989), p. 11.

Chapter

11

Following as Preparation for Leadership

Ken was spending his first afternoon in his new office—the president's office. He had been with his company for eighteen years, and the culmination of his long service was this day, his first day as president and chief executive officer.

Ken began scrolling through the journal he kept on his laptop computer. He was a reflective man, a journal keeper. Just last week, during a brief vacation before beginning his demanding new job, Ken had taken time to try to summarize the high and low points, the formative moments of his career. The first thing he noticed was that Don, the retiring president and CEO, showed up in nearly every entry. Don had been Ken's mentor since the day Ken joined the company.

Ken was just out of college at the time, beginning his first job. Don had left an executive position with a large company to start his own firm. The new company was small and willing to risk hiring a sharp young college grad. On Ken's first day with the company, Don sat him down and explained to him the firm's mission, vision and values. He told Ken his life story, personal dreams and professional hopes. He promised Ken that he would be available for him personally and professionally, and reminded him that the company had high expectations and performance standards. Don concluded his welcoming speech by encouraging Ken to always keep his marriage a top priority.

Through the years, Ken had worked diligently and well, advancing through the ranks of the company, eventually becoming executive vice president and heir apparent to Don as the company grew from start-up to thriving mid-sized business. All the time, Ken watched Don, his mentor and friend.

As Ken reviewed his journal, he begin to categorize, mentally, the things he had learned from Don.

The Values of a Leader

You always knew where you stood with Don. If you were around him long enough, you soon learned where he stood on just about everything.

Like few others Ken had known, Don was a man guided by principles. Only on rare occasions did he articulate those principles, but they were always evident on the surface of his life. He was committed to honesty and integrity in business, to fairness and compassion in his dealings with employees and clients, to deep and loyal friendships, to his faith. He was concerned with truth and justice above all things, but his decisions and judgments were characterized by mercy. He was the same regardless of who he was with or the situation he was in.

He was committed to servant-leadership, to clear vision and thinking and to a focus on developing people. Nothing distracted him from the goals he set, but he was never stuck in his ways. He maintained the posture of a learner and had a free, generous spirit.

A leader has to be a person of firm convictions that reflect a clear direction, a firm purpose and a tender heart for others.

Ken realized that Don had never spelled out his values for him in spite of their many long conversations. Frankly, he wished that Don had been a bit more intentional about communicating his values. But the best lesson in values Ken had learned from Don was that a leader needs to choose and define his values and then let nothing compromise or diminish them. A leader has to be a person of firm convictions that reflect a clear direction, a firm purpose and a tender heart for others.

The Time of a Leader

Building a business was a time-intensive enterprise. In the early days, Ken believed that they couldn't possibly be any busier. They were chronically underfinanced and understaffed. He, Don and the others put in long hours as a matter of course.

As the company grew and thrived, they were able to hire the staff they needed. Ken assumed that Don would have more time on his hands and more freedom to choose what to do with his time. He quickly learned that this was not the case.

Supervising and leading others, setting priorities and direction, being available to mentor and develop others, and building relationships with key clients were tasks that took enormous amounts of time and energy. Don could have worked 100 hours a week, easily.

He didn't, though; Ken got to watch as Don managed his schedule. Don emphasized the big picture, choosing to focus on those tasks that involved the mission and direction of the whole company. He deemphasized urgent but routine matters and spent little time putting out fires. He focused on people, particularly his top managers, insuring that those who worked for him were performing with excellence but were also happy and growing in their lives. He focused on several key results each quarter, subordinating other tasks to insure that he got the outcomes he knew the business needed to continue to grow.

Occasionally, Don would pull Ken aside and counsel him. "Ken, as you grow in responsibility in this company, you're going to see that as a leader you have fewer and fewer choices about how to spend your time and more and more to do.[1] You've got to invest yourself in the tasks that are most critical to our mission and those that achieve the best results. Setting the vision and direction for this company is something that only I can do, so I prioritize that. Always make sure you know what only you can do, then delegate all other tasks and make everything else in your schedule serve that end."

The Priorities of a Leader

Don always seemed to know what he was doing, yet not in an arrogant kind of way. He moved through life with a sense of calm, intense purpose and direction. It appeared that he found it easy to say no to things others would do out of obligation or grudging duty. He was never at a loss for direction, whether the business was growing so fast the company could hardly keep up with it, or in times of struggle and redefinition of the market.

Ken recalled a management team meeting where Don, in an almost off-the-cuff way, spoke of how he set his priorities. "The first thing I do is determine what has to be done, what is required. Some things we don't like to do have to be done because a boss or a board demands them. I do those things as quickly and completely as I can. Then I decide what things will provide the most return on my investment of time and energy. Where will my attention, supervision and resources pay back the highest dividends? Then I plow the best of myself into those things.

"Finally, I determine what will give the greatest rewards. What are the things I enjoy the most and feel the most alive doing? I have learned that if I'm not doing these things then everything else becomes drudgery. I have to find the things that make my heart sing and do them."

People come first.

That day Ken had jotted down in the margins of his calendar: "Priorities: Requirements, Return, Reward." This way of thinking about priorities had served him well for the last decade.[2]

But there was another value that Don lived out in relation to his priorities: *People come first*. He was committed to seeing that the people he led were growing personally and professionally. Often, the company stepped in when an employee's family was in need. Don made sure the company paid for continuing education opportunities for his workers and wrote sincere, glowing references for employees who chose or found it necessary to seek work elsewhere. Don never compromised the mission and vision of the organization. He was not slow to dismiss an employee who was not contributing. But there was never any question that people, and not just profits and accomplishments, were a priority for Don.

The Burdens of a Leader

As Ken looked back on his career, he realized that one assumption about leadership he had held in his early days had been completely overhauled. When he first came to work for Don, to tell the truth, he had assumed that one of the perks of being the boss was getting to do only what you wanted to do. You were paid more, had a bigger office and, best of all, had other people to do your "dirty work." Underlings were the ones to face pressure and deadlines and too-high expectations.

But as Ken watched Don through the years, and as Don opened his heart to Ken, the younger man was impressed with just how much the president carried on his shoulders. Ken came to realize that the pressures and burdens of leadership were formidable.

Don was the court of last appeal for decisions and problems. He was the one required to develop and articulate vision and direction, the one responsible to make key strategic decisions. Middle and even upper management offered advice and counsel, but it was Don's job to synthesize this, weigh it out and make the call. When the company had to lay off workers, it was Don's decision. When the firm faced strained relationships with a union, Don took the heat. The board of directors regarded Don as the one ultimately responsible for progress, results and growth.

Most of all, Ken was impressed with the loneliness of Don's leadership. Often, he would come by the president's office in the early evening and find Don sitting in his half-lit, quiet office, staring reflectively out his window, lost in thought. And Ken was aware that after boisterous, sometimes conflict-filled management team meetings, the other executives would go out together and have fun or complain about the system. Don *was* the system; Ken wondered who he commiserated with, who supported him.

When the other leaders had moved on to the next item, Don was often left to make a final decision, the consequences of which would be his responsibility. Ken knew it was a lonely job.

The Temptations of a Leader

Finally, Ken had journaled about the unique temptations he had observed Don face down. With greater responsibility came greater power, which came with greater financial reward. Don's increased responsibility, power and financial leverage each brought attendant temptations.

Don's wide-ranging responsibilities meant that he was faced with the temptation to identify himself solely with his job. A leader's job is never finished, and Ken had seen other executives—in other businesses and in not-for-profit organizations—become consumed by their work, sometimes sacrificing their health, their friendships and even their families. Often these leaders, in Ken's view, came to believe that the health and well-being of their organization rested on their shoulders alone. Under this kind of pressure, they fell prey to the temptation to become arrogant on the one hand or anxious on the other. Ken had worked with anxious and arrogant managers before, and he knew that nothing could kill leadership credibility faster.

His faith seemed to give him his sense of self and provide his fundamental identity.

Somehow Don had maintained a healthy sense of self, even as his responsibilities grew. He was committed deeply to his job and took responsibility for the organization, but was never consumed by his work. You had the sense that if the worst happened and the business folded, Don would be fine. He found his identity in other things besides his job—as a husband and father, a member of his church, a tennis player and jogger and a community volunteer. His faith, which was deep but never obnoxious, seemed to give him his sense of self and provide his fundamental identity.

The president of a mid-sized business has a moderate degree of power. Don had the ability to hire and fire hundreds of employees. He controlled the allocation of millions of dollars. Because of the company's size and resources, Don could wield significant influence with political and civic leaders. Don was often asked to be on boards and committees; his blessing was considered essential for city council and mayoral candidates. In other words, Don had power.

But he carried his power lightly. To meet Don, you would think he was just an ordinary guy, albeit an articulate one with a strong presence. He rejected the trappings of power, such as elaborate office furnishings, travel perks and special parking spaces. To Ken's knowledge, he had never used his position as head of the company to intimidate, threaten or browbeat any employee. And he managed to be seen as a nonpolitical man, even though he cared deeply about many public policy issues.

It was clear that Don was a man who desired to use his power to accomplish good things and to serve other people. Ken was not sure that Don even realized fully the power that he had.

Don had worked hard through the years and the business had thrived. As a result, his personal income provided him and his family with a more-than-comfortable lifestyle. Don, as the founder and universally respected leader of the company, could set his own level of compensation. But early in his career, he had determined to never receive a salary of more than a certain percentage higher than that of his lowest-paid support staff. Ken knew many CEOs of comparable organizations who made much more than Don did.

While Don took advantage of many of the good things money could buy—a comfortable home and car, occasional vacations and good educational opportunities for his children—he was never preoccupied with his wealth, and he never spent extravagantly. He quietly gave generously to charities and to his church—and he made sure that the company did as well.

In addition, Don instituted strict financial controls and accountability throughout the organization. The company was known for being nearly "fraud-proof" and was respected for its careful accounting and auditing procedures. Don was above reproach when it came to financial management; he managed his money rather than being managed by his money. He used his resources for good things and good causes, while not being afraid to spend a moderate amount for enjoyment and recreation.

Ken leaned back in his office chair and reflected out loud, "Don could have screwed up at a lot of different points in his career. He could have compromised his integrity on a dozen different issues and, in some cases, no one would have objected or even noticed. But he never did." Don was a man of integrity.

A Follower in the Bull Pen

A critical theme in this book has been that followership has great value in itself and is in no way inferior to leadership. Followers should devote themselves to following and not worry about leadership opportunities which may come in the future.

But there is another side to this. Leaders earn the right to be leaders by being exemplary followers first.

And most leaders have a developing sense of call to leadership which precedes the actual call to leadership.

Perhaps you are a follower who feels this call to lead. You are content with where you are now, you're not angling for political advantage or undermining your leader for your own benefit. You are following as best you can.

But you sense that God has called you to leadership and you want to be faithful to that call. How can you use your time as a follower to prepare yourself for future leadership? What can you do now as a follower of competence and integrity to insure that you will be a leader with these same qualities?

Leaders earn the right to be leaders by being exemplary followers first.

Ideally, you have a strong, good leader like Don to look to, a leader who serves as example and mentor. If you don't have a mentor, put this book down—right now—and pray that God will give you one. And make it a matter of continued prayer. A mentor who truly cares for you and does what he can to teach you, to give you opportunities and to provide for your growth is indispensable for your development as a leader.

Earlier I wrote about Coach Dean Smith, the winningest college basketball coach in history. When Coach Smith retired following the 1996-1997 season, his successor was Bill Guthridge, who had been Smith's assistant for more than thirty years. Guthridge's appointment was a surprise to some who had expected one of Smith's younger protégés, who had gone on to become successful head coaches, to get the job. No one had ever paid much attention to Guthridge, a man of few words who had studiously tried to serve his boss in any way he could without seeking personal attention. Not a few predicted the demise of the best college basketball program in the nation.

Coach Guthridge's first team lost only four games and advanced to the Final Four of the NCAA basketball championship. His third team returned to the Final Four. Not exactly a letdown.

As unassuming a head coach as he had been as a three-decades assistant, Guthridge told reporters that he planned to keep a cell phone at the bench so that he could call Smith for advice in the waning moments of close games.

There appear to be two keys to Guthridge's early success. First, he learned from the master coach and applied those lessons. Carolina fans were relieved that the team looked much the same as it did during Smith's nearly four-decade tenure. They emphasize defense first, look to take the ball inside on offense, are unselfish and highly disciplined and emphasize the team over the individual. But astute fans have also noticed that Guthridge's teams are different from Smith's in several respects. Coach Guthridge allows his players a bit more freedom to be creative and expressive on offense. His bench players are a bit more boisterous and demonstrative. He allows his assistants input into practice and game plans, while Smith ran a self-described "benevolent dictatorship." And, perhaps most significantly, he allows freshmen to be significant contributors to the team, something Smith almost never did.

Bill Guthridge's coaching bears the unmistakable imprint of Dean Smith's influence. But he is his own man as well. Guthridge appears to be almost the perfect follower: committing himself to serve and learn from his leader for thirty (!) years, but ready to lead with effectiveness, creativeness and originality when he is called upon to take more responsibility.

> 1. Live a life of investing in others.
> 2. Stay close to Jesus' heart.
> 3. Commit yourself to following well.

Assuming you have a call to leadership and a mentor to help you navigate this call, what should be the themes of your life as a follower? What can you do to insure that, when it is your time to lead, you will be successful and effective as well? I will end this book with three thoughts along these lines.

First, *live a life of investing in others*. Leaders and followers alike are committed to serving and investing in others. Develop the habits of caring for others now, so that it will come naturally to you when you are called upon to lead. Don't be so preoccupied with your own development as a leader that you miss the opportunity to care for others. Leaders who do not put others first are ineffective. Develop the discipline of caring for and prioritizing others now.

Second, *stay close to Jesus' heart.* It is hard work to be a follower, sometimes harder to be a leader. A leader is lonelier, faces greater temptations and is subject to higher levels of attack, spiritually and visibly, than followers. Cultivate a heart of devotion to Jesus now, so that His character is displayed in yours and so that you have adequate reservoirs of spiritual resources and seasoning when your times of leadership testing come.

Third, *commit yourself to following well,* even if leadership never comes. You may have misinterpreted a call to leadership. You may have to wait thirty years. You may be exactly where you are supposed to be for a very long time. Whatever the case, even as you prepare for leadership, follow with the kind of commitment and intensity of someone who never plans on going anywhere else. Follow hard, follow passionately, follow with integrity.

Follow as if the next thing will never come, because it might not. On the other hand, follow with an eye always to the future. Does this sound paradoxical? It should, because it is. This kind of mind-set is what is required to be a fully devoted follower of Jesus, who said that He could return at any moment, but called on us to be about investing our lives in a kingdom that grows slowly over a long period of time.

The Baton Is Passed

It was growing late, and Ken's laptop battery was running low. He exited the program, shut down the machine and closed the lid. He bowed his head and said a quick, heartfelt prayer for wisdom and guidance. When he raised his head and opened his eyes, Don was standing there.

"Don't worry," Don said with a smile. "I won't be hanging around here in your way. I've got better things to do. I just forgot a couple of boxes. And, to be honest, I hoped to find you here."

"Ken," he continued, "you know that I'm not big on speeches. But I did want to tell you one thing. You have served me and this company well for many years. You have paid your dues, put aside your own agenda and ego, and given yourself to a larger cause than your own. In that time, I have watched you grow in confidence and skill. I am so proud of you, and I hope you don't mind my saying that. You are ready to lead this company. The time I have spent with you I regard as my greatest legacy to this company.

"I ask only one thing of you, Ken. Find someone—several people—and invest in them in the same way I have invested in you. Love them, challenge them, make them mad, ask more of them than they think they can accomplish, support them when they fail, give them opportunities including some of your own. Give to them loyalty and time and require that they give you the same. Love them so much and so well that they won't be able to conceive of doing otherwise. Make their hopes and dreams your hopes and dreams. Most of all, serve them from your heart."

Don put his hand for a moment on Ken's shoulder, turned and left the office.

A leader gives to a follower, who becomes a leader, who will give to other followers. Leaders and followers intertwined in community, service and love—may it always be so.

Endnotes

1. See Peter Drucker, *The Executive in Action* (New York: HarperBusiness, 1996), pp. 549-575.
2. John C. Maxwell, *The 21 Irrefutable Laws of Leadership* (Nashville: Thomas Nelson, 1998), pp. 176-178.